Information presented in this course should not be used as

MW01230353

Table of Contents

OREC Code and Rules

This chapter will deal with some of the material covered in the OKLAHOMA REAL ESTATE LICENSE CODE AND RULES. For ease of reading and studying, specific code and rule reference section numbers have been omitted from this text. All students are directed to review the actual code, the most up to date version can be found on the Oklahoma Real Estate Commission's website (http://www.ok.gov/OREC/).

The terms Oklahoma Real Estate Commission, OREC, and Commission are used interchangeably in the course material.

At the end of this chapter, you will be able to:

- Discuss the OREC Code and Rules that deal with the authority of the commission, acts of associates, license requirements, advertising, and aspects of contract law.
- Explain the Code and Rules that deal with disclosure of license status, misrepresentation, the complaint process, duty to account, license transfers, inactive status, and notification requirements.
- Describe the rules that address commission disputes, education requirements, license renewal requirements, causes for suspension or revocation, prohibited dealings, and unlicensed activity.

Key terms and definitions used in this chapter include:

- **Code** – The OKLAHOMA REAL ESTATE LICENSE CODE AND RULES as of November 1, 2017 (See page 27.)

- **Real Estate Broker** – shall include any person, partnership, association or corporation, foreign or domestic, who for a fee, commission or other valuable consideration, or who with the intention or expectation of receiving or collecting a fee, commission or other valuable consideration, lists, sells or offers to sell, buys or offers to buy, exchanges, rents or leases any real estate, or who negotiates or attempts to negotiate any such activity, or solicits listings of places for rent or lease, or solicits for prospective tenants, purchasers or sellers, or who advertises or holds himself out as engaged in such activities.

- **Broker Associate** – shall include any person who has qualified for a license as a broker and who is employed or engaged by, associated as an independent contractor with, or on behalf of, a broker to do or deal in any act, acts or transaction set out in the definition of a broker.

- **Real Estate Sales Associate** – Any person having a renewable license and working for a real estate broker

- **Provisional Sales Associate** – Any person who has been licensed after June 30, 1993, and working for a real estate broker and subject to an additional forty-five-clock-hour post licensing educational requirement to be completed within the twelve-month license term.

- **Promulgate** – To officially put a law into effect

The Oklahoma Real Estate Commission (OREC) has been re-created to continue until July 1, 2017, in accordance with the State's sunset law provisions. OREC has the following features:

- It consists of seven (7) members.
- It has the authority to regulate and issue real estate licenses.
- All members must be citizens of the United States.

- All members must be residents of the State for at least three years prior to their appointment.
- Five members must be licensed real estate brokers and have had at least five (5) years' active experience as real estate brokers prior to their appointment and be engaged full time in the real estate brokerage business.
- One member must be a lay person not in the real estate business.
- One member must be an active representative of a school of real estate located within the State of Oklahoma and approved by the Oklahoma Real Estate Commission.
- No more than two members can be appointed from the same congressional district.
- Members are appointed by the Governor with the advice and consent of the Senate.
- The term of an OREC member is four (4) years.
- Members are entitled to receive travel expense reimbursement.

OREC has the legal status and mandate to:

- Sue and be sued in its official name.
- Affix an official seal to legal documents.
- Report all fees charged, collected and received at the close of each fiscal year with the Governor and State Auditor and Inspector.

OREC has the authority and duty to perform all of the following acts/tasks:

1. Promulgate rules, prescribe administrative fees, and make rules necessary to perform of its duties.

2. Administer license examinations.

3. Sell computer testing and license applications.

4. Issue real estate licenses.

5. Regulate the activities of licensed real estate professionals.

6. Discipline licensees, instructors and real estate schools by one or more of the following actions:

   - Reprimand
   - Probation
   - Additional education requirements
   - License suspension or revocation
   - Fine
   - Disciplinary proceeding
   - Penalty for late license renewal

7. Approve instructors and organizations offering courses of study in real estate.

8. Contract with attorneys and other professionals to carry out the functions and purposes of the Code.

9. Apply for injunctions and restraining orders for violations of the Code.

10. Create an Oklahoma Real Estate Contract Form Committee.

11. Establish reciprocal agreements with other real estate licensing jurisdictions.

12. Designate and employ a hearing examiner or examiners.

13. Require that the burden of proof in any hearing be upon the party that filed the motion.

All acts performed by a broker associate or provisional sales associate under the provisions of the Real Estate License Code must be done **only** in the name of the associate's broker. Associates cannot enter into a brokerage agreement with a party in the associate's name and can only be allowed to enter into the agreement in the name of the broker. A real estate broker may authorize associates to provide brokerage services in the name of the real estate broker as permitted under The Oklahoma Real Estate License Code, which may include the execution of written agreements.

An associate is prohibited from working for more than one broker at the same time, **unless** the associate's broker agreed to loan the associate to another broker for a specific duty to be performed, such as:

- Sitting at an open house
- Calling an auction or performing other auction related duties
- Any other specific duty as requested in writing and approved by the Commission

Note: The employing broker is responsible for all acts performed by the associate while the associate is performing a specific duty for another broker.

An associate is responsible for acts of unlicensed assistants. An associate who employs an unlicensed assistant is responsible in conjunction with the broker for all real estate related activities of the unlicensed assistant.

License Issuance and Changes

Each associate license will be *issued to the associate's broker,* who will keep custody of the license. Upon an associate leaving the association of the broker, his or her license must be returned to the Commission, together with a release executed by the broker.
Any change of association from one firm to another, or relocation from one office to another within a firm by an associate must be filed in the Commission office within ten (10) days.

An active associate transferring from one broker to a new broker may continually act if the change is done in a timely manner and in compliance with the ten (10) day notification requirement.

An associate is required to notify the Commission office of any change in his or her current home address within ten (10) days of change.

OREC has established license requirements for obtaining a broker or broker associate license. See OREC Code and Rules and the following link
https://www.ok.gov/OREC/documents/New%20Broker%20Associate%20Licensure%2011-01-2017.pdf

License Ineligibility

The following persons are ineligible for a license:

- Any applicant convicted of any crimes defined in Section 13.1 of Title 21 of the Oklahoma Statutes is not eligible to obtain a real estate license within twenty (20) years of the completion of any criminal sentence, including parole and probation.
- Any applicant convicted of a felony involving forgery, embezzlement, obtaining money under false pretense, extortion, conspiracy to defraud, fraud, or any other similar offense may not apply for a license within ten (10) years of the completion of any criminal sentence, including parole and probation.
- Any applicant convicted of any other felony cannot obtain a real estate license within five (5) years of the completion of any criminal sentence, including parole and probation.

As with the broker and broker associate license, OREC has established license requirements for obtaining a provisional sales associate license. Each applicant for such a license must:

- Be a person of good moral character, eighteen years of age or older.

- Successfully complete **ninety (90) clock hours** of approved coursework. (Note that this education is *valid for three years* after the school has certified completion. If the applicant has not applied for a license within that period, he or she will have to take another 90 hours of education before applying for a license.)
- Make application on approved OREC forms submitted with the proper examination fee.
- Appear in person to take and successfully complete a real estate license exam.
- Submit to a national criminal history record check.

Once the applicant has passed the examination, received final approval of
the application, and paid the appropriate license fee along with the Oklahoma Real Estate Education and Recovery Fund fee, the Commission will issue the license.

After a provisional sales associate license is issued, the licensee is required to successfully complete **forty-five (45) clock hours** of post-license education prior to the first license expiration date.
The following entities are excluded from the state's real estate license requirements:

- Any party that acquires and or sells real estate based on its own use
- Any entity acting as an attorney-in-fact for the owner or acting for a legally appointed trustee
- Any resident manager hired by the owner or employed by a broker that is engaged in the leasing of property
- Any person engaged by a corporation or governmental body to acquire easements, rights-of-way, leases, permits and licenses
- Any person hired to acquire real estate via eminent domain
- Any resident that receives one hundred dollars or less as a "resident referral fee"
- Any person managing a transient lodging facility
- Any employee working for a broker that manages a state or federal housing subsidized unit

OREC has established the following advertising requirements and prohibitions:

- A broker must use their registered business trade name or the name under which the broker is licensed.
- Yard signs must include the broker's office telephone number and not be used as a "shill" marketing tool.
- A firm cannot register or use a trade name of another licensed firm.
- Advertisement must indicate that the party is a real estate broker and not a private party.
- Firm advertisement must include "agency," "company," "realty," or "real estate," as the case may be. Legible legal abbreviations are acceptable.
- Advertisement with only a post office box number, telephone number, or street address is not acceptable.
- Franchise names must be clearly revealed in all office identification and note that each office is independently owned and operated.
- Advertisement is prohibited that is directed at or referred to persons of a particular race, color, creed, religion, national origin, familial status, or handicap.
- Advertisement is prohibited that is misleading or inaccurate and misrepresents any property, terms, values, services, or policies.
- No property can be advertised for sale, rent, lease, or exchange, unless the broker has first secured the permission of the owner and has a definite date of expiration.
- Social networking advertisement requires licensees to indicate their license status and include their broker's reference contact information.
- Seller incentives are acceptable providing the promotion is clearly disclosed to the public.
- Team names must register with the Commission. See OREC Code and Rules and OREC website for more details.

OREC has established the following advertising requirements and prohibitions for Associates:

- An associate is prohibited from advertising under only the associate's name.

- All advertising must be under the direct supervision of the associate's broker.
- The associate must include the name of the associate's broker or the name under which the broker operates

If approved by the associate's broker, the associate is allowed to use a(n):

- Personal insignia
- Personal nickname or alias which has been registered with the OREC
- Team name (Team name must be registered with the Commission; for more details see OREC Code and Rules and the OREC website.)
- Slogan
- Broker's registered domain/website name which must appear on every individual page and/or frame.
- Associate's contact informational yard sign, provided the registered name or trade name and office telephone number of the broker is included
- Generic open house/directional sign when used in conjunction with broker's signs

A licensee is required to disclose in writing on all documents pertaining to a real estate transaction and in all advertisement that he or she is licensed.

A broker may provide brokerage services to one or both parties in a transaction. A broker who is providing brokerage services to one or both parties must describe and ***disclose in writing*** the broker's duties and responsibilities **prior to** the party or parties signing a contract to sell, purchase, lease, option, or exchange real estate.

A firm that provides brokerage services to both parties in a transaction must give written notice to both parties that the firm is providing brokerage services to both parties **prior to** the parties signing a contract to purchase, lease, option or exchange real estate.

If a broker intends to provide fewer brokerage services than those required to complete a transaction, the broker must provide written disclosure to the party for whom the broker is providing brokerage services. Such disclosure must include a description of those steps in the transaction for which the broker will not provide brokerage services, and also state that the broker assisting the other party in the transaction is not required to provide assistance with these steps in any manner.

According to the Broker Relationships Act effective November 1, 2013:

- The term "brokerage service agreement" means an oral or written agreement to provide brokerage services by a real estate broker to a person who has entered into to a real estate transaction.
- When a firm provides brokerage services to more than one party to the transaction, the broker must provide written notice to those parties that the broker is providing brokerage services to more than one party.

It is recommended that students review the Brokerage Relationships Act in its entirety.

The ***Statute of Frauds*** requires certain types of contracts ***to be in writing*** in order to be enforceable. The statute comes from a 1677 English law that provides the basis for the current requirement. The goal of written contract rules is to avoid fraud by requiring written proof of the underlying agreement.

In Oklahoma, the following types of contracts need to be executed in writing:

- Contracts that take longer than one year to complete
- Agreements to pay another person's debts, with some exceptions
- An agreement made upon consideration of marriage, other than a mutual promise to marry
- Real estate sales or real estate leases for longer than one year (Leases for one year or less may be oral and are enforceable.)

- Contracts establishing a single-party brokerage relationship

Licensees are required to disclose their status as licensees when attempting to purchase property for themselves or for another entity in which the licensee has an interest.

Referrals

No licensee can, without disclosing the fact in writing to all parties on both sides of the transaction:

- Accept or receive any fee, commission, salary, rebate, kickback or other compensation or consideration allowed by law in connection with the recommendation, referral or procurement of any product or service, including financial services.
- Own any beneficial interest in any entity which provides any product or service, including financial services to home owners, home buyers or tenants, in connection with the sale, lease, rental or listing of any real estate.

Activities or interests of associates must be disclosed to his or her broker who has the responsibility to make written disclosures to all parties.

If any associate owns any beneficial interest in any entity which provides any product or service, including financial services, to home owners, home buyers, or tenants, the associate must disclose the nature and extent of the interest to his or her broker. The obligation to make such disclosure is a continuing one.

Beneficial interest disclosures must be made either:

- Prior to or at the time that any recommendation, referral or procurement of any product or service is made or
- At or before the time that it becomes apparent to the licensee that any entity in which the licensee owns any beneficial interest may provide any product or service

Substantial misrepresentation covers a wide area of misbehavior and inappropriate actions. The Code does not describe all possible types. However, the Code does identify the following key areas of concern:

- A licensee using a fictitious or false instrument for the purpose of inducing a lender to give a mortgage or insure any type of real estate loan
- Failure to disclose to a buyer or other cooperative licensee or firm any known material defects
- A broker trading on the name of a revoked or suspended licensee
- A licensee making verbal statements or falsifying documents that inflate the true and actual sales price of a property or stating terms, verbally or in writing, that differ from those actually agreed upon by the parties to the transaction

Complaints may be filed by the public or by the Commission's own motion. Once filed the following process will take place:

- A complaint notice will be sent immediately to the subject licensee or unlicensed person.
- The complaint recipient will be required to file an adequate written response within fifteen (15) days of the notice.
- Subsequent to the fifteen (15) day answer period, an investigation will be conducted to ascertain whether or not charges should be lodged and a formal hearing ordered.
- At the completion of the investigation a written report is submitted to the Commission.
- The Commission will then determine whether or not the evidence warrants formal charges and, if so, will order a hearing.
- If a formal hearing is ordered, all parties will receive copies of any written report accompanied by the findings, if any. The Commission must provide at least a fifteen (15) day written hearing notice to parties in the complaint.

- If the Commission finds that public health, safety, or welfare is in jeopardy, emergency action can be taken to order a summary suspension of a licensee pending proceedings for revocation or other action within thirty (30) days. The summary suspension will remain in effect until further order by the Commission.

Broker

A licensee is responsible to account for all non-owned valuables that transfer into his or her possession as a result of a real estate transaction. Following is a list of major duties and responsibilities as noted in the Code:

- A broker must deposit all checks and monies belonging to others in a separate account in a financial institution wherein the deposits are insured by an agency of the federal government.
- The broker is required to be a signor on the account.
- The account must be a trust account in the name of the broker as it appears on the license or trade name as registered with the Commission
- All escrow funds must be deposited before the end of the third banking day following acceptance of an offer, unless otherwise agreed to in writing by all parties.
- The broker must maintain funds in the trust account until the transaction is consummated or terminated and proper accounting is made.
- At all times, the broker must maintain an accurate and detailed record of all funds thereof.

Deposit funds are referred to, but not limited to:

- Earnest money deposits
- Money received upon final settlements
- Rents and security deposits
- Money advanced in the payment of closing expenses
- Money advanced for expenditures on behalf of subject principal

Associate

The sales associate is:
- Required to turn over all documents, files and monies deposited, payments made, or things of value received by the associate to his or her broker promptly
- Required to deliver a copy of all transaction instruments to the appropriate parties in the transaction
- Not authorized to open or maintain a trust or escrow account

In the event of a dispute, the broker must retain escrow money or valuables until he or she has a written release from all parties consenting to its disposition or until a civil action is filed to determine its disposition at which time he or she may pay or turn it in to the court.

In the absence of a pending civil action and upon the passage of thirty (30) days from the date of final termination of the contract, the broker may disburse escrow monies or valuables to either purchaser or seller based on a good decision by the broker that the opposite party has failed to perform the agreed upon action. Disbursement can be made after fifteen (15) days written notice to all parties concerned.

Following are key trust account management Code policies and rules:

- Commingling of broker funds is prohibited. However, deposits of personal funds necessary to service the account are acceptable.
- An interest bearing account is acceptable, but it must be disclosed in writing to all parties that the account bears interest and must identify the party receiving the interest. The Commission does not prohibit the broker from

receiving the earned interest. The broker is required to maintain complete and accurate records of the interest earned. The interest bearing account must be a demand type account.

- A Broker is not required to open a trust account unless funds or items are held in escrow.
- All trust type accounts must be registered with Commission.
- A broker must inform the Commission in writing of any accounts which are closed and no longer in use.
- A broker must furnish a signed settlement statement regarding each consummated real estate transaction.
- A broker must pay over all sums of money held in escrow after the closing of any transaction.
- In the event a transaction does not consummate, a broker must promptly disburse the earnest money or items to the proper party in accordance with the terms of the contract.

The Code defines the following rules regarding record retention:

- A broker must maintain a bookkeeping system with all documents that accurately and clearly disclose all trust account documents.
- A broker must maintain all records and files for a minimum of **five (5) years** after consummation or termination of a transaction.
- Records can be stored on alternative media as defined as an electronic device used to store or retrieve information.
- Trust account records must be maintained in their original format for a minimum of **two (2) years**. Trust account records may then be transferred to an alternative media for the remaining required retention time.
- Records, with the exception of trust account records, may be transferred at any time to an alternative media for the remaining required retention time.
- After documents are converted to alternative media, a quality assurance check must be done to ensure that every document was imaged and can be reproduced in a legible and readable condition on a display device.
- After the quality assurance check is completed, the original documents may be destroyed.
- A broker must maintain the proper technology to view, retrieve, and print all records.

Each associate license is issued to the associate's broker, who will retain custody of the license. Upon an associate leaving the broker, the associate's license must be returned to the Commission along with a release executed by the broker.

Any firm change or relocation from one office to another within a firm by an associate must be filed in the Commission office within ten (10) days. The associate's new broker will be required to file a consent agreement to sponsor the associate on a form provided by the Commission. An associate requesting an association or office change is required to pay a fee of $25.

A previous broker may pay compensation due a disassociated associate directly to the associate and not be required to make the payment through the associate's new broker. However, any agreements between the associate and prior broker requiring further activities to be performed in connection with the compensation to be received can only be performed with consent and acknowledgment of the new broker.

A licensee who fails to comply with all Code and Rule requirements for active license status is placed on inactive status. Upon compliance, a licensee will be approved for active status.

The Commission may place a license on inactive status when the request is accompanied by sufficient reason. A provisional sales associate or sales associate licensee can request to be placed on inactive status by completing the appropriate OREC form and paying a fee. Following are other rules that apply:

- While on inactive status, the person is required to pay regular renewal fees. **Note:** During active military service, a licensee is not required to pay the fees but must request the inactive status prior to each term for which the license is to be issued.

- When a person is ready to re-activate the license, he or she will be required to complete the appropriate form, remit the required fee, and may be subject to meeting continuing education requirements before the license can be activated.

There are several instances when a licensee must make notification to the Commission.

- Every licensed person must notify the Commission in writing of the conviction or plea of guilty or nolo contendere to any felony offense within thirty (30) days after the plea is taken and also within thirty (30) days of the entering of an order of judgment and sentencing.
- Each licensee is ultimately responsible to the Commission to furnish evidence of having successfully completed the continuing education requirements for license renewal, activation, or reinstatement.
- Each provisional sales associate shall be responsible to furnish evidence to the Commission of having successfully completed a Commission approved forty-five (45) clock hour post-license education course or its equivalent.
- Any change of association from one firm to another, or relocation from one office to another within a firm by an associate must be filed in the Commission office within ten (10) days.
- An associate is required to notify the Commission office of his or her current home address. If the licensee moves, the address change must be filed in the Commission office within ten (10) days of the change.
- Any change of name of a licensee or licensed firm must be filed in the Commission office within ten (10) days of such change.

As mentioned on a previous screen, the Commission has some notification requirements towards licensees.

- If a complaint is filed against a licensee, the Commission must send a complaint notice to the person immediately.
- If a formal hearing is ordered, the Commission must provide at least a fifteen (15) day written hearing notice to all parties in the complaint.

The Commission does not establish the rate of commissions to be charged for real estate services and has no interest therein. Any disputes that arise between brokers regarding commission are usually handled by the local Association of REALTORS®.

Programs to handle such disputes include:

- **Negotiation** – This is the direct bargaining between two parties to a dispute where they attempt to resolve the dispute without the intervention of others.
- **Mediation** – A neutral third party assists the disputants in negotiating a mutually acceptable settlement. Mediators do not render decisions but help to facilitate the parties to the dispute to come to their own agreement by clarifying issues, utilizing persuasion and other conflict resolution strategies.
- **Arbitration** – Parties agree to submit existing or future disputes to a neutral third party, an arbitrator, who will decide how the dispute will be resolved. In binding arbitration, that decision is a final resolution of the dispute. In non-binding arbitration, the parties elect whether to settle with the arbitrator's decision or to continue on to litigation.

As we mentioned on an earlier screen, an applicant for licensure as a provisional sales associate must successfully complete at least ninety (90) clock hours of instruction or its equivalent as determined by the Commission. The pre-license course of study is referred to as the **Basic Course of Real Estate, Part I of II.**

After receiving his or her license, a provisional sales associate is required to successfully complete forty-five (45) clock hours of post-license education prior to the first license expiration date. This course of study is referred to as the **Provisional Post-license Course of Real Estate, Part II of II.**

The licensee is responsible for notifying the Commission of training completion. A provisional sales associate who fails to complete the post-license education requirement prior to the first expiration date of the provisional sales associate license will not be entitled to renew the license.

Also as we mentioned on an earlier screen, an applicant for licensure as a broker must successfully complete at least ninety (90) clock hours of instruction or its equivalent as determined by the Commission. This course of study is referred to as the **Advanced Course in Real Estate**.

As a condition for renewing a license, licensees are required to complete continuing education hours within the thirty-six (36) months immediately preceding the term for which the license is to be issued. The required number of continuing education hours for a licensee is as follows:

- As a condition of a license activation or active reinstatement, each license with an expiration date of June 30, 2014 and thereafter must provide evidence of completion of twenty-one (21) clock hours of Commission approved subject matter. These hours must have been taken in the same license term for which the license is to be issued, with the exception of a licensee whose hours were not used in the preceding license term. In that case, the hours taken in the preceding license term shall count towards an applicable license activation or active reinstatement.
- Of the requires twenty-one (21) clock hours of continuing education, six (6) clock hours must consist of required subject matter.
- The required subject matter consists of at least one (1) clock hour in all of the following subjects each license term: **Professional Conduct, Broker Relationships Act, Fair Housing, Contracts and Forms, Code and Rule Updates and Current Issues.** The remaining fifteen (15) clock hours may consist of elective subject matter as approved by the Commission.
- Any licensee may complete the Broker in Charge course consisting of fifteen (15) clock hours in lieu of the required subject matter.
- Any Broker who holds or has held a license type of Broker Manager (BM), Proprietor Broker (BP), or Branch Broker (BB) during any portion of their current license term is required to successfully complete the 15-hour Broker in Charge course. In addition, such broker must complete at least two (2) of the six (6) required subject matter courses listed above.
- Any broker that lapsed or renewed inactive in their previous license term or current license term who applies for reinstatement or activation and held in their previous or current license term the license type of Broker Manager (BM), Proprietor Broker (BP), or Branch Broker (BB) must complete the Broker in Charge course and two (2) of the six (6) required subject matter equal to at least six (6) hours prior to their license being reinstated active or reactivating.

The following offerings will **not** be considered by the Commission to meet continuing education requirements:
- General training or education not directly related to real estate
- Business skills training such as typing, speed reading, memory improvement, report writing, and personal motivation
- Sales promotion or other meetings held in conjunction with the general real estate brokerage business
- Meetings which are a normal part of in-house training
- That portion of any training devoted to breakfast, luncheon, dinner, or other refreshments
- Pre-license training to obtain a provisional sales associate or sales associate license or license examination refresher courses

The Commission may, upon its own motion and/or upon a written complaint filed by any person, investigate the business transactions of any real estate licensee. The following acts will be investigated:

- Making a materially false or fraudulent statement in an application for a license
- Making substantial misrepresentations or false promises in the conduct of business

- Accepting compensation as a real estate associate from a real estate broker who is not the associate's employing broker
- Representing a real estate broker other than the broker with whom the associate is associated without the express knowledge and consent of the broker with whom the associate is associated
- Failing, within reasonable time, to account for transaction monies, property and/or documents
- Paying compensation to any person for services performed in violation of the Code
- Acting in an untrustworthy, improper, fraudulent, or dishonest manner
- Disregarding any Code provisions
- Guaranteeing future profits which may result from the resale of real estate
- Advertising any real estate without the consent of the owner
- Soliciting buyers by offering "free lots," conducting lotteries, contests, or prizes or offering prizes for the purpose of influencing a purchaser or prospective purchaser of real estate
- Accepting employment or compensation for appraising real estate contingent upon the reporting of a predetermined value or issuing any appraisal report on real estate in which the licensee has an interest unless the licensee's interest is disclosed in the report
- Paying compensation to a non-licensed individual
- Being convicted of, or pleaded guilty or nolo contendere to a crime involving moral turpitude
- Commingling funds
- Being convicted in a court of violating provisions of the federal fair housing laws
- Failing to render an accounting and pay others their earned commission
- Being convicted of the crime of forgery, embezzlement, obtaining money under false pretenses, extortion, conspiracy to defraud, fraud, or any similar offense
- Advertising to buy, sell, rent, or exchange any real estate without disclosing that the licensee is a real estate licensee
- Paying any part of a fee, commission, or other valuable consideration received by a real estate licensee to any person not licensed
- Offering to loan, pay or make it appear that a down payment or earnest money has been made in a transaction deposit for a purchaser or seller in connection with the real estate transaction
- Violating the Residential Property Condition Disclosure Act

A suspended/revoked licensee must return their license certificate and pocket identification card to the Commission office **on or before the date the suspension/revocation becomes effective**.

A person cannot file an application for reissuance of a license after revocation of the license **within three (3) years** of the effective date of revocation.

The Code prohibits licensees from untrustworthy, improper, fraudulent or dishonest dealing with the public, customers and clients. In addition, the following behaviors and actions have been identified as prohibited:

- Making a brokerage service contract without a date of termination
- Purchasing of property by a licensee for himself or herself or another entity in which the licensee has an interest without first making full disclosure and obtaining the approval of the owner, if such property is listed with the broker or the broker's firm
- Making repeated misrepresentations, even if not fraudulent, occurring as a result of the licensee not keeping informed of pertinent facts concerning a property
- Procuring the signature to a purchase offer which has no definite purchase price or no method of payment, termination date, possession date or property description
- Paying any fees with an insufficient funds check
- Lending a broker's license to an associate, permitting an associate to operate as a broker, or failing to properly supervise the activities of an associate
- Failing to disclosure in writing that a licensee has an interest in the property he or she is selling

- Failing to inform buyers and/or sellers in writing at the time an offer is presented that certain closing costs and brokerage service fees are to be paid and the approximate amount of those costs
- Failing to comply with a written demand from the Commission to respond to a complaint in writing, or to disclose any information within the licensee's knowledge, or to produce any document, book or record in the licensee's possession or under the licensee's control
- Failing to put an offer in writing at the request of a proposed purchaser
- Failing to submit all bonafide offers to a seller when such offers are received prior to the seller accepting an offer in writing
- Engaging in any conduct in a real estate transaction which demonstrates bad faith or incompetency
- Failing to act, in marketing the licensee's own property, with the same good faith as when acting in the capacity of a real estate licensee
- Intentionally acting in the capacity of a broker or branch office broker when licensed as an associate
- Discouraging a party from obtaining an inspection on a property
- Allowing access to, or control of, real property without the owner's authorization
- Knowingly providing false or misleading information to the Commission during the course of an investigation
- Interfering with an OREC investigation
- Knowingly cooperating with an unlicensed person or entity to perform licensed real estate activities
- Failing to disclose any immediate family relationships to all parties in the transaction
- Failing as a broker to ensure all persons performing real estate licensed activities under the broker are properly licensed
- Allowing an associate to perform licensed activities outside the broker's supervision
- Failing to maintain trust account documents

It is unlawful for any person to act as a real estate licensee or to hold himself or herself out as such, unless the person has been licensed to do so under the OREC Code.

No person whose license is revoked or suspended can operate directly or indirectly or have a participating interest, or act as a member, partner or officer, in any real estate business, corporation, association or partnership that is required to be licensed.

No person whose license is canceled, surrendered, or lapsed pending investigation or disciplinary proceedings can operate directly or indirectly or have a participating interest, or act as a member, partner or officer, in any real estate business, corporation, association or partnership that is required to be licensed.

Any unlicensed person who violates real estate law may be guilty of a misdemeanor punishable by a fine of not more than One Thousand Dollars ($1,000.00), or by imprisonment in the county jail for not more than six (6) months, or by both such fine and imprisonment.

In addition, after notice and hearing, and upon finding a violation of the Code, the Commission may impose a fine of not more than Five Thousand Dollars ($5,000.00) or the amount of the commission earned, whichever is greater for each violation of the Code for unlicensed activity.

All collected funds must be deposited in the Oklahoma Real Estate Education and Recovery Fund.

Oklahoma Brokerage Relationships

Introduction and Objectives

The Oklahoma Brokerage Relationships Act which went into effect in November 2000 has undergone some changes effective as of November 1, 2013 that could make your job significantly easier. The new changes provide a well-thought-out legal framework around which brokers can tailor their specific business models.

In this course we'll examine those recent law changes and also review those parts of the law that have not changed.

At the end of this unit, you will be able to:

- Discuss the duties and responsibilities of brokers as they exist today.
- Explain what brokerage services are owed to the parties when a single firm or a single licensee provides services to both parties.
- Describe other new changes in the law as well as those provisions that have not changed.

Review of Definitions

Before we discuss the specific provisions of the law, let's review some of the terms defined in the law. Section 858-351 of the Brokerage Relationships Act lists the following terms and their intended definitions.

- **Broker** means a real estate broker, an associated broker associate, sales associate, or provisional sales associate authorized by a real estate broker to provide brokerage services.
- **Brokerage services** means those services provided by a broker to a party in a transaction.
- **Party** means a person who is a seller, buyer, landlord, or tenant or a person who is involved in an option or exchange.
- **Transaction** means an activity or process to buy, sell, lease, rent, option or exchange real estate. Such activities or processes may include, without limitation, soliciting, advertising, showing or viewing real property, presenting offers or counteroffers, entering into agreements, and closing such agreements.
- **Firm** means a sole proprietor, corporation, association, or partnership.

Overview of the Changes

Before we delve into the details, here's a short synopsis of the important changes to this law.

- The terms single-party broker and transaction broker have gone away.
- The duties and responsibilities that were previously designated as belonging to transaction brokers are now "assigned" to all brokers.
- The rules on confidentiality have expanded to include information specifically designated by the party as being confidential.
- All brokerage services agreements must contain the list of those broker duties and responsibilities. However a broker can choose to add to that list and provide more services. Alternatively, a broker can choose to offer fewer services as long as he or she tells the client in writing what services will not be provided.
- Any individual broker or any firm can assist both parties to a transaction, as long as the broker or firm gives the parties written notice and gets a written confirmation of that disclosure from the parties.

As we said at the start of the course, these changes have the potential to make your job easier. So now let's take a look at the changes in more detail.

Broker Duties and Responsibilities

As a licensee, you have certain responsibilities to the parties that you serve. Even if you do not have a formal written brokerage services agreement with a party, you still owe that party some specific duties and responsibilities.

As listed in section 858-353 of the Brokerage Relationships Act, you owe the following duties to all parties *regardless of whether or not you have a brokerage services agreement in place.* **Please Note:** These duties are mandatory and you cannot waive, ignore, or otherwise do away with them in any way (with the exception of the second bullet as noted below).

- Treat all parties with honesty and exercise reasonable skill and care.
- Unless *specifically waived in writing by a party* to the transaction:
    - Receive all written offers and counteroffers.
    - Reduce offers or counteroffers to a written form upon the request of any party to a transaction.
    - Present all written offers and counteroffers in a timely manner.
- Account for all money and property received by the broker in a timely manner.
- Keep any and all confidential information that you receive from **a party or prospective party** confidential. We'll discuss confidentiality in more detail on upcoming screens.
- Disclose information pertaining to the property as required by the Residential Property Condition Disclosure Act.
- Comply with all requirements of the Oklahoma Real Estate License Code and all applicable statutes and rules.

Broker Duties and Responsibilities to Clients

In addition to the duties and responsibilities that we listed on the previous screen, a broker has the following duties and responsibilities **only** to a party for whom he or she is providing brokerage services in a transaction. These duties are also **mandatory**, so you may not waive, ignore, or otherwise do away with them in any way.

- You must inform the party in writing *when an offer is made* that the party will be expected to pay certain costs and brokerage service costs and you must provide the approximate amount of those costs.

    What this means is that you must provide a *seller's net sheet* to any seller for whom you are providing brokerage services and you must provide an *estimate of closing costs* for any buyer to whom you are providing brokerage services.
- You must keep the party informed regarding the transaction.

Note: When a licensee or a firm **works with both parties to a transaction**, the broker duties and responsibilities listed on this and the previous screen will remain in place for **both parties**.

Confidentiality

As we said on a previous screen, you **must not disclose** any of the confidential information given to you by **any** party. You or your firm cannot disclose such information without the consent of the party disclosing the information unless one of the following three situations exists:

- The party or prospective party disclosing the information gives consent to the disclosure **in writing**.
- The disclosure is **required by law**.
- The information is made public or becomes public as the result of actions from a source **other than the firm**.

According to the law, the following information must be considered confidential and will be the **only** information considered confidential in a transaction:

- That a party or prospective party is willing to pay more or accept less than what is being offered.
- That a party or prospective party is willing to agree to financing terms that are different from those offered.
- The motivating factors of the party or prospective party purchasing, selling, leasing, optioning, or exchanging the property.
- Information *specifically designated as confidential by a party (or prospective party)* unless such information is public.

  Since this type of information is not as straightforward as the previous three types of information, it is crucial for you have a conversation with your client regarding what he or she considers confidential information. Your client will be sharing lots of information with you during the course of your relationship and you need to be clear about which of that information the client feels is confidential. You need to explain to your client that aside from pricing, financing, and motivation issues, all other shared information is "fair game" to be disclosed or shared with other parties, ***unless the client clearly instructs you to keep specific pieces of information confidential.***

Confidentiality Examples

Since confidentiality is so important, let's look at some situations and see where confidentiality may be or may not be an issue.

Example 1:

Broker Sam is working with seller Tim. Sam and Tim agree to list his home for $200,000, but Tim tells Sam he would be willing to accept up to $25,000 less. Because this information is a specific ***pricing*** issue, this is definitely confidential information and Sam must not disclose it to anyone.

Example 2:

Broker Mary is working with Seller Theresa. Theresa tells Mary that she has not paid her real estate taxes for the past two years. Mary can disclose this information to any prospective buyers she works with because it is not confidential information. Information about the payment of real estate taxes is in the ***public record*** and available to anyone who wants to look for it.

Example 3:

Broker Gail is showing homes to Buyers Rick and Sandy, but they do no have a written brokerage services agreement. They find a home on which they want to make an offer. Rick tells Gail that he has just been transferred from another state and is already living in an apartment. They need the deal to close quickly so Sandy doesn't have to continue living alone in another state with the children. Because this information is a specific ***motivating factors*** issue, this is definitely confidential information and Gail must not disclose it to the listing broker.

Example 4:

Broker Dan is working with Seller Sally. Sally tells Dan that the roof has been leaking and there have been water spots on the upstairs bathroom and bedroom ceilings, but she sprays the spots with bleach when they appear so they're not noticeable. Sally tells Dan to keep this information confidential. When Dan checks the Property Disclosure document, he does not find any information about the leaking roof. Dan cannot keep this information confidential because material defects that affect property condition are **required by law to be disclosed**.

Example 5:

Broker Alan is working with Buyer Grace. Grace is a long-time employee of a large company and makes a considerable salary. Grace tells Alan that she does not want anyone to know where she works for fear that they will think she has the financial ability to pay any amount for a home. Even though a party's employment location is technically not confidential information, Grace has designated it as confidential, so Alan cannot disclose it. As we said earlier, one of the types of confidential information is **information specifically designated as confidential by a party**.

Example 6:

Buyer Brenda is working with Broker Matt and she finds a home on which she is interested in writing an offer. She is a veteran and wants to make an offer using VA financing. However, Brenda tells Matt that she has enough money for a 20% down payment and could do a conventional loan if the VA financing doesn't come through. Because this information is a specific *financing* issue, this is definitely confidential information and Matt must not disclose it.

Brokerage Services Agreements

As we said earlier, *brokerage services* are those services provided by a broker to a party (consumer) in a transaction.

According to the Oklahoma license code, the term **brokerage service agreement** means "*an oral or written agreement to provide brokerage services entered into by a real estate broker and a person who is a party to a real estate transaction and shall include, but not be limited to, listing agreements, buyer broker agreements and property management agreements.*"

So in effect, a brokerage service agreement converts the party or consumer with whom you are working into a client.

Even though this law stipulates that a brokerage service agreement can be oral, good practice dictates that you have all agreements in writing, so as to be clear about the specific duties you will be providing to your clients and to avoid any misunderstandings as the relationship moves along.

All brokerage agreements must incorporate as material terms those duties and responsibilities that we listed on a previous screen as broker duties and responsibilities owed to all parties.

Please Note: All brokerage agreements signed into effect prior to November 1, 2013 do not terminate as of November 1. They stay in effect until the termination date indicated on the agreement, but would need to be amended to comply with the new law. Therefore, instead of "extending" or "amending" existing agreements as you may have done in the past, your clients might be better served to enter into new agreements using the new forms for those agreements that expire after November 1. Using the new forms will minimize confusion for both you and your clients.

Providing Brokerage Services to Both Parties

A **broker** may provide brokerage services to **one or both** parties in a transaction. When a broker provides brokerage services, either to one party or to both parties, he or she must describe and disclose **in writing** those broker's duties and responsibilities we listed earlier **prior to** *the party or parties signing a contract to sell, purchase, lease, option, or exchange real estate.*

Oklahoma Brokerage Relationships

When a **firm** provides brokerage services to **both** parties in a transaction, the firm must provide **written notice to both parties** that the firm is providing brokerage services to both parties ***prior to*** *the parties signing a contract to purchase, lease, option, or exchange real estate.*

In addition, when a firm is providing services to both sides of the transaction, the firm must *ensure that it is complying* with all the broker duties and responsibilities owed to each of the parties as we have discussed throughout this course, as well as all the other requirements of the License Code and Rules.

If a broker intends to provide *fewer brokerage services* than those required to complete a transaction, the broker must provide ***written disclosure*** to the party for whom the broker is providing brokerage services. In the disclosure, the broker must include a description of those steps in the transaction for which he or she will <u>not</u> provide brokerage services. The broker must also state that the broker assisting the other party in the transaction is not required to provide assistance with these steps in any manner.

Confirmation of Disclosures

When a broker is providing brokerage services which he or she must disclose in writing as we described on the previous screen, the parties to whom the broker is providing those brokerage services must confirm in writing that they received the disclosure from the broker.

The parties must provide that confirmation in a separate provision or document that is either incorporated into or attached to the contract to purchase, lease, option, or exchange real estate.

In those cases where a broker is involved in a transaction but he or she ***does not prepare the contract*** to purchase, lease, option, or exchange real estate, the broker must document that he or she has complied with the disclosure requirements.

Note: There is not currently a standard disclosure form that is required or mandated for brokers to use. However, in the past similar forms have been created by the Oklahoma Real Estate Contract Form Committee and approved by the Oklahoma Real Estate Commission. You may see such a form become available for use after November 1, 2013. You can check on the OREC website or check with your local Board of Realtors® for a form that your employing broker may want to adopt for use in your firm.

Other Law Changes

Single Party Broker and Transaction Broker

The terms "single party broker" and "transaction broker" have been eliminated from the law. However, please note that you are not prohibited from using these terms in any brokerage agreements you enter into after November 1, 2013. That being said, if you choose to use either of these terms, you must clearly define the term you use, since it is no longer defined in the law. This could prove to be a confusing task, so you may be best served to refrain from using these terms altogether.

Authority of Broker Associates

This section of the law (Section 858-363) was expanded to include a clearer description of an associate's authority. The additions to this section are indicated in bold. It now reads as follows:

"Each broker associate, sales associate, and provisional sales associate shall be associated with a real estate broker. **Associates shall not enter into a brokerage agreement with a party in the associate's name and shall only be allowed to enter into the agreement in the name of the real estate broker.** *A real estate broker may authorize associates to provide brokerage services in the name of the real estate broker* **as permitted under The Oklahoma Real Estate License Code, which may include the execution of written agreements."**

Amendments to Previous Laws

Two sections of the law remain the same as its previous version, but have been amended.

Broker Compensation – Determination of Relationship –Breach of Duty

Section 858-359(A), as before, stresses that compensation does not determine the relationship a broker has to a party. Subsections B and C have been newly added. The section now reads as follows:

"A. The payment or promise of payment or compensation by a party to a broker does not determine what relationship, if any, has been established between the broker and a party to a transaction.

B. In the event a broker receives a fee or compensation from any party to the transaction based on a selling price or lease cost of a transaction, such receipt does not constitute a breach of duty or obligation to any party to the transaction.

C. Nothing in this section requires or prohibits a broker from charging a separate fee or other compensation for each duty or other brokerage services provided during a transaction."

Abrogation of Common Law Principles of Agency – Remedies Cumulative

Section 858-360(A), as before, indicates that the broker duties and responsibilities specified in this law take precedence over any other fiduciary duties that are based on the common law principles of agency. Subsections B and C have been newly added. The section now reads as follows:

"A. The duties and responsibilities of a broker specified in Sections 858-351 through 858-363 of The Oklahoma Real Estate License Code shall replace and abrogate the fiduciary or other duties of a broker to a party based on common law principles of agency. The remedies at law and equity supplement the provisions of Sections 858-351 through 858-363 of The Oklahoma Real Estate License Code.

B. A broker may cooperate with other brokers in a transaction. Pursuant to Sections 858-351 through 858-363 of The Oklahoma Real Estate License Code, a broker shall not be an agent, subagent, or dual agent and an offer of subagency shall not be made to other brokers.

C. Nothing in this act shall prohibit a broker from entering into an agreement for brokerage services not enumerated herein so long as the agreement is in compliance with this act, the Oklahoma Real Estate Code and the Oklahoma Real Estate Commission Administrative Rules."

What Remains Intact

Not everything in the Oklahoma Broker Relationships Act has changed; some sections have remained essentially the same as before.

Duties of Broker Following Termination, Expiration or Completion of Performance

Oklahoma Brokerage Relationships

This section of the law (Section 858-358) remains exactly the same as it was previously. The intent is very clear and it reads as follows:

"Except as may be provided in a written brokerage agreement between the broker and a party to a transaction, the broker owes no further duties or responsibilities to the party after termination, expiration, or completion of performance of the transaction, except:

- *To account for all monies and property relating to the transaction; and*
- *To keep confidential all confidential information received by the broker during the broker's relationship with a party."*

Use of "Agent" in Trade Name

This section (Section 858-361) has also remained intact, although slightly expanded. The addition to this section is indicated in bold. It now reads as follows:

"A real estate broker and the associates of a real estate broker are permitted under the provisions of this title to use the word "agent" in a trade name **and as a general reference for designating themselves as real estate licensees.***"*

Vicarious Liability

The intent of this section of the law (Section 858-362) did not change. However, it was rewritten to delete the term "transaction broker" from the paragraph. The law now reads as follows:

"A party to a real estate transaction shall not be vicariously liable for the acts or omissions of a real estate licensee who is providing brokerage services under
Sections 858-351 through 858-363 of The Oklahoma Real Estate License Code."

Review

A broker owes the following duties to all parties *regardless of whether or not a brokerage services agreement is in place*:

- Treat all parties with honesty and exercise reasonable skill and care.
- Unless *specifically waived in writing by a party* to the transaction:
    - Receive all written offers and counteroffers.
    - Reduce offers or counteroffers to a written form upon the request of any party to a transaction.
    - Present all written offers and counteroffers in a timely manner.
- Account for all money and property received by the broker in a timely manner.
- Keep any and all confidential information that you receive from **a party or prospective party** confidential.
- Disclose information pertaining to the property as required by the Residential Property Condition Disclosure Act.
- Comply with all requirements of the Oklahoma Real Estate License Code and all applicable statutes and rules.

A broker owes **two additional duties** to a party for whom he or she is providing brokerage services in a transaction:

- Inform the party in writing *when an offer is made* that the party will be expected to pay certain costs and brokerage service costs and provide the approximate amount of those costs.
- Keep the party informed regarding the transaction.

A broker or firm cannot disclose confidential information without the consent of the party disclosing the information unless one of the following three situations exists:

- The party or prospective party disclosing the information gives consent to the disclosure **in writing**.
- The disclosure is **required by law**.
- The information is made public or becomes public as the result of actions from a source **other than the firm**.

According to the law, the following information must be considered confidential and will be the **only** information considered confidential in a transaction:

- That a party or prospective party is willing to pay more or accept less than what is being offered.
- That a party or prospective party is willing to agree to financing terms that are different from those offered.
- The motivating factors of the party or prospective party purchasing, selling, leasing, optioning, or exchanging the property.
- Information *specifically designated as confidential by a party (or prospective party)* unless such information is public.

Even though the law stipulates that a brokerage service agreement can be oral, good practice dictates that a broker have all agreements in writing, so as to be clear about the specific duties he or she will be providing to clients.

When providing brokerage services, either to one party or to both parties, a broker or firm must describe and disclose **in writing** the broker's duties and responsibilities *prior to the party or parties signing a contract to sell, purchase, lease, option, or exchange real estate.*

The parties must then confirm **in writing** that they received the disclosure in a separate provision or document that is either incorporated into or attached to the contract to purchase, lease, option, or exchange real estate.

The terms "single party broker" and "transaction broker" have been eliminated from the law. However, a broker or firm is not prohibited from using those terms in any brokerage agreement entered into after November 1, 2013.

Oklahoma Brokerage Relationships

Not everything in the Oklahoma Broker Relationships Act has changed; some sections have remained essentially the same as before:

- Duties after termination or completion of a transaction
  - Accounting for money and property
  - Maintaining confidentiality

Use of the term "agent" in a trade name and as a general reference for designating brokers as real estate licensees

The Oklahoma Real Estate License Code

§59-858-101. Title and construction.

This Code shall be known and cited as "The Oklahoma Real Estate License Code".

Laws 1974, c. 121, § 101, operative July 1, 1974.

§59-858-102. Definitions.

When used in this Code, unless the context clearly indicates otherwise, the following words and terms shall be construed as having the meanings ascribed to them in this section:

1. The term "real estate" shall include any interest or estate in real property, within or without the State of Oklahoma, whether vested, contingent or future, corporeal or incorporeal, freehold or nonfreehold, and including leaseholds, options and unit ownership estates to include condominiums, time-shared ownerships and cooperatives; provided, however, that the term "real estate" shall not include oil, gas or other mineral interests, or oil, gas or other mineral leases; and provided further, that the provisions of this Code shall not apply to any oil, gas, or mineral interest or lease or the sale, purchase or exchange thereof;

2. The term "broker" shall include any person, partnership, association or corporation, foreign or domestic, who for a fee, commission or other valuable consideration, or who with the intention or expectation of receiving or collecting a fee, commission or other valuable consideration, lists, sells or offers to sell, buys or offers to buy, exchanges, rents or leases any real estate, or who negotiates or attempts to negotiate any such activity, or solicits listings of places for rent or lease, or solicits for prospective tenants, purchasers or sellers, or who advertises or holds himself out as engaged in such activities. "Broker" shall be limited to the license types of Broker Manager (BM), Proprietor Broker (BP) or Branch Broker (BB) as defined in the Code;

3. The term "broker associate" shall include any person who has qualified for a license as a broker associate, and who is employed or engaged by, associated as an independent contractor with, or on behalf of and with the permission of a broker to perform any act set out in the definition of a broker;

4. The term "real estate sales associate" shall include any person having a renewable license and employed or engaged by, or associated as an independent contractor with, or on behalf of, a broker to do or deal in any act, acts or transactions set out in the definition of a broker;

5. "Provisional sales associate" shall include any person who has been licensed after June 30, 1993, employed or engaged by, or associated as an independent contractor with, or on behalf of, a broker to do or deal in any act, acts or transactions set out in the definition of a broker and subject to an additional forty-five-clock-hour postlicensing educational requirement to be completed within the first twelve-month license term. However, the Oklahoma Real Estate Commission shall promulgate rules for those persons called into active military service for purposes of satisfying the postlicensing educational requirement. The license of a provisional sales associate shall be nonrenewable unless the postlicensing requirement is satisfied prior to the expiration date of the license. Further, the terms sales associate and provisional sales associate shall be synonymous in meaning except where specific exceptions are addressed in the Oklahoma Real Estate License Code;

6. The term "successful completion" shall include prelicense, postlicense, and distance education courses in which an approved public or private school entity has examined the individual, to the satisfaction of the entity and standards as established by the Commission, in relation to the course material presented during the offering;

7. The term "renewable license" shall refer to a broker, broker associate or sales associate who is a holder of such license or to a provisional sales associate who has completed the educational requirements within the required time period as stated in the Code;

8. The term "nonrenewable license" shall refer to a provisional sales associate who is the holder of such license and who has not completed the postlicense educational requirement within the required time period as stated in the Code;

9. The term "surrendered license" shall refer to a real estate license which is surrendered, upon the request of the licensee, due to a pending investigation or disciplinary proceedings;

10. The term "canceled license" shall refer to a real estate license which is canceled, upon the request of the licensee and approval of the Commission, due to a personal reason or conflict;

11. "Licensee" shall include any person who performs any act, acts or transactions set out in the definition of a broker and licensed under the Oklahoma Real Estate License Code;

12. The word "Commission" shall mean the Oklahoma Real Estate Commission;

13. The word "person" shall include and mean every individual, partnership, association or corporation, foreign or domestic;

14. Masculine words shall include the feminine and neuter, and the singular includes the plural; and

15. The word "associate" shall mean a broker associate, sales associate or provisional sales associate.

§59-858-201. Oklahoma Real Estate Commission.

A. There is hereby re-created, to continue until July 1, 2017, in accordance with the provisions of the Oklahoma Sunset Law, the Oklahoma Real Estate Commission, which shall consist of seven (7) members. The Commission shall be the sole governmental entity, state, county or municipal, which shall have the authority to regulate and issue real estate licenses in the State of Oklahoma.

B. All members of the Commission shall be citizens of the United States and shall have been residents of the State of Oklahoma for at least three (3) years prior to their appointment.

C. Five members shall be licensed real estate brokers and shall have had at least five (5) years' active experience as real estate brokers prior to their appointment and be engaged full time in the real estate brokerage business. One member shall be a lay person not in the real estate business, and one member shall be an active representative of a school of real estate located within the State of Oklahoma and approved by the Oklahoma Real Estate Commission.

D. No more than two members shall be appointed from the same congressional district according to the latest congressional redistricting act. However, when congressional districts are redrawn, each member appointed prior to July 1 of the year in which such modification becomes effective shall complete the current term of office and appointments made after July 1 of the year in which such modification becomes effective shall be based on the redrawn districts. No appointments may be made after July 1 of the year in which such modification becomes effective if such appointment would result in more than two members serving from the same modified district.

§59-858-202. Appointment - Tenure - Vacancies - Removal.

A. Members of the Oklahoma Real Estate Commission shall be appointed by the Governor with the advice and consent of the Senate.

B. Members of the Commission shall serve until their terms expire. The terms of the Commission members shall be for four (4) years and until their successors are appointed and qualified.

C. Each successor member and any vacancy which may occur in the membership of the Commission shall be filled by appointment of the Governor with the advice and consent of the Senate.

D. The Governor may select appointees from a list of at least three qualified persons submitted by the Oklahoma Association of Realtors, Incorporated.

E. Each person who shall have been appointed to fill a vacancy shall serve for the remainder of the term for which the member whom he will succeed was appointed and until his successor, in turn, shall have been appointed and shall have qualified.

F. Members of the Commission may be removed from office by the Governor for inefficiency, neglect of duty or malfeasance in office in the manner provided by law for the removal of officers not subject to impeachment.

§59-858-203. Compensation of Commissioners.

Each member of the Oklahoma Real Estate Commission shall be entitled to receive travel expenses essential to performing the duties of his office, as provided in the State Travel Reimbursement Act.

§59-858-204. Officers - Employees - Duties and compensation - Meetings.

A. The members of the Commission, within thirty (30) days after their appointment, shall organize and elect a chairman and vice-chairman. Annually thereafter the offices of chairman and vice-chairman shall be attained through election by Commission members.

B. The Commission, as soon after the election of the chairman and vice-chairman as practicable, shall employ a secretary-treasurer and such clerks and assistants as shall be deemed necessary to discharge the duties imposed by the provisions of this Code, and shall determine their duties and fix their compensation subject to the general laws of this state.

C. The chairman of the Commission, and in his absence the vice-chairman, shall preside at all meetings of the Commission and shall execute such duties as the Commission, by its rules, shall prescribe.

D. The secretary-treasurer shall keep a complete and permanent record of all proceedings of the Commission and perform such other duties as the Commission shall prescribe.

§59-858-205. Oklahoma Real Estate Commission Revolving Fund.

A. There is hereby created in the State Treasury a revolving fund for the Oklahoma Real Estate Commission, to be designated the "Oklahoma Real Estate Commission Revolving Fund". The fund shall consist of all monies received by the Oklahoma Real Estate Commission other than the Oklahoma Real Estate Education and Recovery Fund fees or appropriated funds. The revolving fund shall be a continuing fund not subject to fiscal year limitations and shall be under the control and management of the Oklahoma Real Estate Commission.

B. The Oklahoma Real Estate Commission may invest all or part of the monies of the fund in securities offered through the "Oklahoma State Treasurer's Cash Management Program". Any interest or dividends accruing from the securities and any monies generated at the time of redemption of the securities shall be deposited in the General Operating Fund of the Oklahoma Real Estate Commission. All monies accruing to the credit of the fund are hereby appropriated and may be budgeted and expended by the Oklahoma Real Estate Commission.

C. Expenditures from this fund shall be made pursuant to the purposes of this Code and without legislative appropriation. Warrants for expenditures shall be drawn by the State Treasurer based on claims signed by an authorized employee or employees of the Oklahoma Real Estate Commission and approved for payment by the Director of the Office of Management and Enterprise Services.

§59-858-206. Suits - Service - Seal - Certified copies - Location of office.

A. The Commission may sue and be sued in its official name, and service of summons upon the secretary-treasurer of the Commission shall constitute lawful service upon the Commission.

B. The Commission shall have a seal which shall be affixed to all licenses, certified copies of records and papers on file, and to such other instruments as the Commission may direct, and all courts shall take judicial notice of such seal.

C. Copies of records and proceedings of the Commission and all papers on file in the office, certified under the seal, shall be received as evidence in all courts of record.

D. The office of the Commission shall be at Oklahoma City, Oklahoma.

§59-858-207. Annual report of fees.

The Commission shall at the close of each fiscal year file with the Governor and State Auditor and Inspector a true and correct report of all fees charged, collected and received during the previous fiscal year, and shall pay into the General Revenue Fund of the State Treasury ten percent (10%) of the license fees collected and received during the fiscal year.

§59-858-208. Powers and duties of Commission.

The Oklahoma Real Estate Commission shall have the following powers and duties:

1. To promulgate rules, prescribe administrative fees by rule, and make orders as it may deem necessary or expedient in the performance of its duties;

2. To administer examinations to persons who apply for the issuance of licenses;

3. To sell to other entities or governmental bodies, not limited to the State of Oklahoma, computer testing and license applications to recover expended research and development costs;

4. To issue licenses in the form the Commission may prescribe to persons who have passed examinations or who otherwise are entitled to such licenses;

5. To issue licenses to and regulate the activities of real estate brokers, provisional sales associates, sales associates, branch offices, nonresidents, associations, corporations, and partnerships;

6. Upon showing good cause as provided for in The Oklahoma Real Estate License Code, to discipline licensees, instructors and real estate school entities by:
    a. reprimand,

   b. probation for a specified period of time,

   c. requiring education in addition to the educational requirements provided by Section 858-307.2 of this title,

   d. suspending real estate licenses and approvals for specified periods of time,

   e. revoking real estate licenses and approvals,

   f. imposing administrative fines pursuant to Section 858-402 of this title, or

   g. any combination of discipline as provided by subparagraphs a through f of this paragraph;

7. Upon showing good cause, to modify any sanction imposed pursuant to the provisions of this section and to reinstate licenses;

8. To conduct, for cause, disciplinary proceedings;

9. To prescribe penalties as it may deem proper to be assessed against licensees for the failure to pay the license renewal fees as provided for in this Code;

10. To initiate the prosecution of any person who violates any of the provisions of this Code;

11. To approve instructors and organizations offering courses of study in real estate and to further require them to meet standards to remain qualified as is necessary for the administration of this Code;

12. To contract with attorneys and other professionals to carry out the functions and purposes of this Code;

13. To apply for injunctions and restraining orders for violations of the Code or the rules of the Commission;

14. To create an Oklahoma Real Estate Contract Form Committee by rule that will be required to draft and revise real estate purchase and/or lease contracts and any related addenda for voluntary use by real estate licensees;

15. To enter into contracts and agreements for the payment of food and other reasonable expenses as authorized in the State Travel Reimbursement Act necessary to host, conduct, or participate in meetings or training sessions as is reasonable for the administration of this Code;

16. To conduct an annual performance review of the Executive Director and submit the report to the Legislature; and

17. To enter into reciprocal agreements with other real estate licensing regulatory jurisdictions with equivalent licensing, education and examination requirements.

§59-858-209. Compliance with the Administrative Procedures Act.

A. In the exercise of all powers and the performance of all duties provided in this Code, the Commission shall comply with the procedures provided in the Administrative Procedures Act. Appeals shall be taken as provided in said act.

B. The Commission may designate and employ a hearing examiner or examiners who shall have the power and authority to conduct such hearings in the name of the Commission at any time and place subject to the provisions of this section and any applicable rules or orders of the Commission. No person shall serve as a hearing examiner in any proceeding in which any party to the proceeding is, or at any time has been, a client of the hearing examiner or of any firm, partnership or corporation with which the hearing examiner is, or at any time has been, associated. No person who acts as a hearing examiner shall act as attorney for the Commission in any court proceeding arising out of any hearing in which he acted as hearing examiner.

C. In any hearing before the Commission, the burden of proof shall be upon the moving party.

§59-858-301. License required – Exceptions.

It shall be unlawful for any person to act as a real estate licensee, or to hold himself or herself out as such, unless the person shall have been licensed to do so under the Oklahoma Real Estate License Code. However, nothing in this section shall:

1. Prevent any person, partnership, trust, association or corporation, or the partners, officers or employees of any partnership, trustees or beneficiaries of any trust, association or corporation, from acquiring real estate for its own use, nor shall anything in this section prevent any person, partnership, trust, association or corporation, or the partners, officers or employees of any partnership, trustees or beneficiaries of any trust, association or corporation, as owner, lessor or lessee of real estate, from selling, renting, leasing, exchanging, or offering to sell, rent, lease or exchange, any real estate so owned or leased, or from performing any acts with respect to such real estate when such acts are performed in the regular course of, or as an incident to, the management, ownership or sales of such real estate and the investment therein;

2. Apply to persons acting as the attorney-in-fact for the owner of any real estate authorizing the final consummation by performance of any contract for the sale, lease or exchange of such real estate;

3. In any way prohibit any attorney-at-law from performing the duties of the attorney as such, nor shall this Code prohibit a receiver, trustee in bankruptcy, administrator, executor, or his or her attorney, from performing his or her duties, or any person from performing any acts under the order of any court, or acting as a trustee under the terms of any trust, will, agreement or deed of trust;

4. Apply to any person acting as the resident manager for the owner or an employee acting as the resident manager for a licensed real estate broker managing an apartment building, duplex, apartment complex or court, when such resident manager resides on the premises and is engaged in the leasing of property in connection with the employment of the resident manager;

5. Apply to any person who engages in such activity on behalf of a corporation or governmental body, to acquire easements, rights-of-way, leases, permits and licenses, including any and all amendments thereto, and other similar interests in real estate, for the purpose of, or facilities related to, transportation, communication services, cable lines, utilities, pipelines, or oil, gas, and petroleum products;

6. Apply to any person who engages in such activity in connection with the acquisition of real estate on behalf of an entity, public or private, which has the right to acquire the real estate by eminent domain;

7. Apply to any person who is a resident of an apartment building, duplex, or apartment complex or court, when the person receives a resident referral fee. As used in this paragraph, a "resident referral fee" means a nominal fee not to exceed One Hundred Dollars ($100.00), offered to a resident for the act of recommending the property for lease to a family member, friend, or coworker;

8. Apply to any person or entity managing a transient lodging facility. For purposes of this paragraph, "transient lodging facility" means a furnished room or furnished suite of rooms which is rented to a person on a daily basis, not as a principal residence, for a period less than thirty (30) days; or

9. Apply to employees of a licensed real estate broker who lease residential housing units only to eligible persons who qualify through a state or federal housing subsidized program to lease the property in an affordable housing development project. "Affordable housing development project" means a housing development of four or more units constructed for lease to specifically eligible persons as required by the particular federal or state housing program, including, but not limited to, the U.S. Department of Housing and Urban Development, the U.S. Department Agriculture Rural Development, the U.S. Department of Treasury Internal Revenue Service, or the Oklahoma Housing Finance Agency.

§59-858-301.1. Eligibility for license - Applicants convicted of criminal offenses - Time periods for disqualification - Procedure.

A. Any applicant convicted of any crimes defined in Section 13.1 of Title 21 of the Oklahoma Statutes shall not be eligible to obtain a real estate license within twenty (20) years of the completion of any criminal sentence, including parole and probation.

B. Any applicant convicted of a felony involving forgery, embezzlement, obtaining money under false pretense, extortion, conspiracy to defraud, fraud, or any other similar offense or offenses shall not be eligible to obtain a real estate license within ten (10) years of the completion of any criminal sentence, including parole and probation.

C. Any applicant convicted of any other felony shall not be allowed to obtain a real estate license within five (5) years of the completion of any criminal sentence, including parole and probation.

D. For the purposes of this section, the term "applicant" shall mean any person making an application for original licensure as a provisional sales associate, sales associate, broker associate, or broker, and shall not apply to any licensee seeking renewal of a current license.

E. Any applicant with a felony conviction shall not automatically receive a license after the timelines set forth in this section, but may be licensed in accordance with the licensing provisions set forth in the Oklahoma Real Estate License Code and Rules.

§59-858-301.2. Notification of Commission of conviction or plea of guilty or nolo contendere to felony offense.

Every licensed person pursuant to the provisions of the Oklahoma Real Estate License Code shall notify the Commission in writing of the conviction or plea of guilty or nolo contendere to any felony offense within thirty (30) days after the plea is taken and also within thirty (30) days of the entering of an order of judgment and sentencing. Added by Laws 2009, c. 133, § 2, eff. Nov. 1, 2009.

§59-858-302. Eligibility for license as provisional sales associate - Qualifications - Examination - Posteducation requirement.

A. Any person of good moral character, eighteen (18) years of age or older, and who shall submit to the Commission evidence of successful completion of ninety (90) clock hours or its equivalent as determined by the Commission of basic real estate instruction in a course of study approved by the Commission, may apply to the Commission to take an examination for the purpose of securing a license as a provisional sales associate. The education required in this subsection shall only be valid for a period of three (3) years from the date the school certified successful completion of the course; thereafter, the applicant shall be required to successfully complete an additional ninety (90) clock hours or its equivalent in basic real estate instruction.

B. Application shall be made upon forms prescribed by the Commission and shall be accompanied by an examination fee as provided for in this Code and all information and documents the Commission may require.

C. The applicant shall appear in person before the Commission for an examination which shall be in the form and inquire into the subjects the Commission shall prescribe.

D. If it shall be determined that the applicant shall have passed the examination, received final approval of the application, and paid the appropriate license fee provided for in this Code along with the Oklahoma Real Estate Education and Recovery Fund fee, the Commission shall issue to the applicant a provisional sales associate license.

E. Following the issuance of a provisional sales associate license, the licensee shall then submit to the Commission, prior to the expiration of the provisional license, evidence of successful completion of forty-five (45) clock hours or its equivalent as determined by the Commission of postlicense education real estate instruction in a course(s) of study approved by the Commission. A provisional sales associate who fails to submit evidence of compliance with the postlicense education requirement pursuant to this section, prior to the first expiration date of the provisional sales associate license, shall not be entitled to renew such license for another license term. However, the Commission shall promulgate rules for those persons called into active military service for purposes of satisfying the postlicense education requirement.

§59-858-303. Eligibility for license as real estate broker or broker associate - Examination.

A. Applicants for a broker license who hold a sales associate license or are not currently licensed shall meet the following requirements:
1. Be persons of good moral character who have had two (2) years' licensure within the previous five (5) years or its equivalent;
2. Submit to the Commission evidence of successful completion of ninety (90) clock hours or its equivalent as determined by the Commission of advanced real estate instruction in a course of study approved by the Commission and completion of the Broker in Charge course as defined in the Code. The education required in this subsection shall only be valid for a period of three (3) years from the date the school certified successful completion of the course; thereafter, the applicant shall be required to successfully complete an additional ninety (90) clock hours or its equivalent in advanced real estate instruction;
3. Provide documentation verifying ten real estate transactions within the past five (5) years or the equivalent as determined by the Commission. For the purposes of this subsection, transaction shall be defined in Section 858-351 of this title and shall be demonstrated on forms developed by the Commission; and
4. Apply to the Commission to take an examination for the purpose of securing a license as a broker.

B. Application shall be made upon forms prescribed by the Commission and shall be accompanied by fees as provided for in this Code and all information and documents the Commission may require.

C. If the applicant has passed the examination, received final approval of the application, and paid the appropriate fees provided for in this Code along with the Oklahoma Real Estate Education and Recovery Fund fee, the Commission shall issue to the applicant a broker license.

D. Applicants for a broker license who hold a broker associate license shall meet the following requirements:
1. Be persons of good moral character who have had two (2) years' licensure within the previous five (5) years, or its equivalent;
2. Submit to the Commission evidence of successful completion of the Broker in Charge course as defined in the Code; and
3. Provide documentation verifying ten real estate transactions within the past five (5) years or the equivalent as determined by the Commission. For the purposes of this subsection, transaction shall be defined in Section 858-351 of this title and shall be demonstrated on forms developed by the Commission.

E. Application shall be made upon forms prescribed by the Commission and shall be accompanied by fees as provided for in this Code and all information and documents the Commission may require.

F. If the applicant has received final approval of the application, and paid the appropriate fee provided for in this Code along with the Oklahoma Real Estate Education and Recovery Fund fee, the Commission shall issue to the applicant a broker license.

§59-858-303A

A. Applicants for a broker associate license shall meet the following requirements:
1. Be persons of good moral character who hold a renewable broker associate or sales associate license and who have had two (2) years' licensure within the previous five (5) years as a sales associate or provisional sales associate, or its equivalent;
2. Submit to the Commission evidence of successful completion of ninety (90) clock hours, or its equivalent as determined by the Commission, of advanced real estate instruction in a course of study approved by the Commission. The education required in this subsection shall only be valid for a period of three (3) years from the date the school certified successful completion of the course; thereafter, the applicant shall be required to successfully complete an additional ninety (90) clock hours or its equivalent in advanced real estate instruction; and
3. Apply to the Commission to take an examination for the purpose of securing a license as a broker associate.

B. Application shall be made upon forms prescribed by the Commission and shall be accompanied by fees as provided for in this Code and all information and documents the Commission may require.

C. The applicant shall appear in person for an examination which shall be prescribed by the Commission.

D. If the applicant has passed the examination, received final approval of the application, and paid the appropriate fees provided for in this Code along with the Oklahoma Real Estate Education and Recovery Fund fee, the Commission shall issue to the applicant a broker associate license.

§59-858-303B. Accounting of expenditure for services.

Any real estate broker who charges and collects any fees in advance of the services provided by the broker shall provide a detailed accounting of expenditures to the person such services are performed for within ten (10) days after the time specified to perform such services or upon written request from person for whom services are performed for, but no longer than one (1) year from date of contract for such services.
Added by Laws 1985, c. 231, § 6, operative July 1, 1985.

§59-858-304. Evidence of successful completion of basic or advanced real estate instruction - Syllabus of instruction.

A. A certified transcript from an institution of higher education, accredited by the Oklahoma State Regents for Higher Education or the corresponding accrediting agency of another state, certifying to the successful completion of a six-academic-hour basic course of real estate instruction, or its equivalent, for which college credit was given, shall be prima facie evidence of successful completion of the clock hours of basic real estate instruction for a provisional sales associate applicant as required in Section 858-302 of this Code. The education required in this subsection shall only be valid for a period of three (3) years from the date the school certified successful completion of the course; thereafter, the applicant shall be required to successfully complete an additional six-academic-hour basic course of real estate instruction, or its equivalent.

B. A certified transcript from an institution of higher education, accredited by the Oklahoma State Regents for Higher Education or the corresponding accrediting agency of another state, certifying to the successful completion of a three-academic-hour course of real estate instruction, or its equivalent, consisting of the provisional sales associate postlicense education requirements for which college credit was given, shall be prima facie evidence of successful completion of the clock hours of real estate instruction for the postlicense education requirement as required in Section 858-302 of this title.

C. A certified transcript from an institution of higher education, accredited by the Oklahoma State Regents for Higher Education or the corresponding agency of another state, certifying to the successful completion of a six-academic-hour advanced course of real estate instruction, or its equivalent, for which college credit was given, shall be prima facie evidence of successful completion of the clock hours of advanced real estate instruction, or its equivalent, as required in Section 858-303 of this Code for a broker applicant.

D. Each school, whether public or private other than institutions of higher education, must present to the Commission its syllabus of instruction, prior to approval of such school.

§59-858-305. Licensing of associations, corporations and partnerships.
   A. The Oklahoma Real Estate Commission may license as a broker any association or corporation in which the managing member or managing officer holds a license as a real estate broker, as defined in this Code, and in which every member, officer or employee who acts as a real estate broker or real estate sales associate holds a license for that purpose, as defined in this Code. The Commission may license as a real estate broker any partnership in which each partner holds a license as a real estate broker, as defined in this Code.
   B. The Oklahoma Real Estate Commission shall require the registration of all teams affiliated under a brokerage for the purpose of allowing the Commission to better align and track the teams within each brokerage. For the purposes of this section, a team shall mean any two or more licensees who work under the supervision of the same broker, work together on real estate transactions to provide brokerage services, represent themselves to the public as being part of a team, and are designated by a team name. Such registration shall occur before a team performs any licensed activities, and the broker shall notify the Commission when any team name is no longer being used. The Commission may charge a registration fee for each team not to exceed the administrative costs of the registration process.
   C. Application for licenses and registrations described in this section shall be made on forms prescribed by the Commission and shall be issued pursuant to rules promulgated by the Commission.

§59-858-306. Licensing of nonresidents.
   A. Any person who desires to perform licensed activities in Oklahoma but maintains a place of business outside of Oklahoma may obtain an Oklahoma nonresident license by complying with all applicable provisions of this Code including the successful completion of the applicable Oklahoma state portion of the real estate examination.
   B. The nonresident shall give written consent that actions and suits at law may be commenced against the nonresident licensee in any county in this state wherein any cause of action may arise or be claimed to have arisen out of any transaction occurring in the county because of any transactions commenced or conducted by the nonresident or the nonresident's associates or employees in such county. The nonresident shall further, in writing, appoint the secretary-treasurer of said Commission as service agent to receive service of summons for the nonresident in all of such actions and service upon the secretary-treasurer of such Commission shall be held to be sufficient to give the court jurisdiction over the nonresident in all such actions.
   C. A broker who is duly licensed in another state and who has not obtained an Oklahoma nonresident license may enter a cooperative brokerage agreement with a licensed real estate broker in this state. If, however, the broker desires to perform licensed activities in this state, the broker must obtain an Oklahoma nonresident license.

§59-858-307.1. Issuance of license - Term - Fees.
   A. The Oklahoma Real Estate Commission shall issue every real estate license for a term of thirty-six (36) months with the exception of a provisional sales associate license whose license term shall be for twelve (12) months. License terms shall not be altered except for the purpose of general reassignment of the terms which might be necessitated for maintaining an equitable staggered license term system. The expiration date of the license shall be the end of the twelfth or thirty-sixth month, whichever is applicable, including the month of issuance. Fees shall be promulgated by rule, payable in advance, and nonrefundable.
   B. If a license is issued for a period of less than thirty-six (36) months, the license fee shall be prorated to the nearest dollar and month. If a real estate sales associate or a provisional sales associate shall qualify for a license as a real estate broker, then the real estate provisional sales associate's or sales associate's license fee for the remainder of the license term shall be prorated to the nearest dollar and month and credited to such person's real estate broker's license fee.

§59-858-307.2. Renewal of license - Continuing education requirement.

A. Beginning November 1, 2004, as a condition of renewal or reactivation of the license, each licensee with the exception of those exempt as set out in this section shall submit to the Oklahoma Real Estate Commission evidence of completion of a specified number of hours of continuing education courses approved by the Commission, within the thirty-six (36) months immediately preceding the term for which the license is to be issued. The number of hours, or its equivalent, required for each licensed term shall be determined by the Commission and promulgated by rule. Each licensee shall be required to complete and include as part of said continuing education a certain number of required subjects as prescribed by rule.

B. The continuing education courses required by this section shall be satisfied by courses approved by the Commission and offered by:

1. The Commission;
2. A technology center school;
3. A college or university;
4. A private school;
5. The Oklahoma Association of Realtors, the National Association of Realtors, or any affiliate thereof;
6. The Oklahoma Bar Association, American Bar Association, or any affiliate thereof; or
7. An education provider.

C. The Commission shall maintain a list of courses which are approved by the Commission.

D. The Commission shall not issue an active renewal license or reactivate a license unless the continuing education requirement set forth in this section is satisfied within the prescribed time period.

E. The provisions of this section do not apply:

1. During the period a license is on inactive status;
2. To a licensee who holds a provisional sales associate license;
3. To a nonresident licensee licensed in this state if the licensee maintains a current license in another state or states and has satisfied the continuing education requirement for license renewal in that state or states. If the nonresident licensee is exempt from the continuing education requirements in all states where the nonresident holds a license, the nonresident licensee shall successfully complete this state's continuing education requirement for license renewal or reactivation; or
4. To a corporation, association, partnership or branch office.

§59-858-307.3. Application for reissuance of license after revocation.

A person shall not be permitted to file an application for reissuance of a license after revocation of the license within three (3) years of the effective date of revocation.

§59-858-307.4. Criminal history record - Investigation - Costs.

A. Prior to the issuance of a license pursuant to this Code, each applicant shall submit to a national criminal history record check, as defined by Section 150.9 of Title 74 of the Oklahoma Statutes.

B. Upon receipt by the Commission of criminal history, the Commission shall conduct an investigation in accordance with rules promulgated by the Commission.

C. The costs associated with the national criminal history record check shall be paid by the applicant.

§59-858-308. Current list of licensees.

In the interest of the public, the Commission shall keep a current list of the names and addresses of all licensees, and of all persons whose licenses have been suspended or revoked, together with such other information relative to the enforcement of the provisions of this Code as it may deem advisable and desirable. Such listings and information shall be a matter of public record.

§59-858-309. Inactive status for licensees.

A. The Commission may place a license on inactive status when the request therefor is accompanied by sufficient reason; however, said status shall not relieve the licensee from paying the required fees. The request for inactive status shall be in writing on forms furnished by the Commission.

B. During active military service, any licensee shall not be required to pay the fees but shall request the inactive status prior to each term for which the license is to be issued.

§59-858-310. Location of office - Licenses for branch offices.
   A. A real estate broker shall maintain a specific place of business. Such place of business shall comply with all local laws and shall be available to the public during reasonable business hours.
   B. If a real estate broker maintains more than one place of business and the additional location is an extension of the main office, a branch office license must be obtained for each additional location. Each branch office shall be under the direction and supervision of a separate broker and shall be considered a managing broker of the branch office. Application shall be made upon forms as prescribed by the Commission.

§59-858-311. Action not maintainable without allegation and proof of license.
   No person, partnership, association or corporation acting as a real estate licensee shall bring or maintain an action in any court in this state for the recovery of a money judgment as compensation for services rendered in listing, buying, selling, renting, leasing or exchanging of any real estate without alleging and proving that such person, partnership, association or corporation was licensed when the alleged cause of action arose.
   Added by Laws 1974, c. 121, § 311, operative July 1, 1974. Amended by Laws 1998, c. 60, § 17, eff. Jan. 1, 1999.

§59-858-312. Investigations - Cause for suspension or revocation of license.
   The Oklahoma Real Estate Commission may, upon its own motion, and shall, upon written complaint filed by any person, investigate the business transactions of any real estate licensee, and may, upon showing good cause, impose sanctions as provided for in Section 858-208 of this title. Cause shall be established upon the showing that any licensee has performed, is performing, has attempted to perform, or is attempting to perform any of the following acts:
   1. Making a materially false or fraudulent statement in an application for a license;
   2. Making substantial misrepresentations or false promises in the conduct of business, or through real estate licensees, or advertising, which are intended to influence, persuade, or induce others;
   3. Failing to comply with the requirements of Sections 858-351 through 858-363 of this title;
   4. Accepting a commission or other valuable consideration as a real estate associate for the performance of any acts as an associate, except from the real estate broker with whom the associate is associated;
   5. Representing or attempting to represent a real estate broker other than the broker with whom the associate is associated without the express knowledge and consent of the broker with whom the associate is associated;
   6. Failing, within a reasonable time, to account for or to remit any monies, documents, or other property coming into possession of the licensee which belong to others;
   7. Paying a commission or valuable consideration to any person for acts or services performed in violation of the Oklahoma Real Estate License Code;
   8. Any other conduct which constitutes untrustworthy, improper, fraudulent, or dishonest dealings;
   9. Disregarding or violating any provision of the Oklahoma Real Estate License Code or rules promulgated by the Commission;
   10. Guaranteeing or having authorized or permitted any real estate licensee to guarantee future profits which may result from the resale of real estate;
   11. Advertising or offering for sale, rent or lease any real estate, or placing a sign on any real estate offering it for sale, rent or lease without the consent of the owner or the owner's authorized representative;
   12. Soliciting, selling, or offering for sale real estate by offering "free lots", conducting lotteries or contests, or offering prizes for the purpose of influencing a purchaser or prospective purchaser of real estate;
   13. Accepting employment or compensation for appraising real estate contingent upon the reporting of a predetermined value or issuing any appraisal report on real estate in which the licensee has an interest unless the licensee's interest is disclosed in the report. All appraisals shall be in compliance with the Oklahoma real estate appraisal law, and the person performing the appraisal or report shall disclose to the employer whether the person performing the appraisal or report is licensed or certified by the Oklahoma Real Estate Appraiser Board;
   14. Paying a commission or any other valuable consideration to any person for performing the services of a real estate licensee as defined in the Oklahoma Real Estate License Code who has not first secured a real estate license pursuant to the Oklahoma Real Estate License Code;
   15. Unworthiness to act as a real estate licensee, whether of the same or of a different character as specified in this section, or because the real estate licensee has been convicted of, or pleaded guilty or nolo contendere to, a crime involving moral turpitude;

16. Commingling with the licensee's own money or property the money or property of others which is received and held by the licensee, unless the money or property of others is received by the licensee and held in an escrow account that contains only money or property of others;

17. Conviction in a court of competent jurisdiction of having violated any provision of the federal fair housing laws, 42 U.S.C. Section 3601 et seq.;

18. Failure by a real estate broker, after the receipt of a commission, to render an accounting to and pay to a real estate licensee the licensee's earned share of the commission received;

19. Conviction in a court of competent jurisdiction in this or any other state of the crime of forgery, embezzlement, obtaining money under false pretenses, extortion, conspiracy to defraud, fraud, or any similar offense or offenses, or pleading guilty or nolo contendere to any such offense or offenses;

20. Advertising to buy, sell, rent, or exchange any real estate without disclosing that the licensee is a real estate licensee;

21. Paying any part of a fee, commission, or other valuable consideration received by a real estate licensee to any person not licensed;

22. Offering, loaning, paying, or making to appear to have been paid, a down payment or earnest money deposit for a purchaser or seller in connection with a real estate transaction; and

23. Violation of the Residential Property Condition Disclosure Act.

§59-858-312.1. Certain persons prohibited from participation in real estate business.

A. No person whose license is revoked or suspended shall operate directly or indirectly or have a participating interest, or act as a member, partner or officer, in any real estate business, corporation, association or partnership that is required to be licensed pursuant to this Code.

B. No person whose license is cancelled, surrendered or lapsed pending investigation or disciplinary proceedings shall operate directly or indirectly or have a participating interest, or act as a member, partner or officer, in any real estate business, corporation, association or partnership that is required to be licensed pursuant to this Code until such time as the Commission makes a determination on the pending investigation or disciplinary proceedings and approves an application for license.

§59-858-313. Confidential materials of the Commission.

The following materials of the Commission are confidential and not public records:

1. Examinations conducted by the Commission and materials related to the examinations; and

2. Educational materials submitted to the Commission by a person or entity seeking approval and/or acceptance of a course of study.

§59-858-351. Definitions.

Unless the context clearly indicates otherwise, as used in Sections 858-351 through 858-363 of The Oklahoma Real Estate License Code:

1. "Broker" means a real estate broker, an associated broker associate, sales associate, or provisional sales associate authorized by a real estate broker to provide brokerage services;

2. "Brokerage services" means those services provided by a broker to a party in a transaction;

3. "Party" means a person who is a seller, buyer, landlord, or tenant or a person who is involved in an option or exchange;

4. "Transaction" means an activity or process to buy, sell, lease, rent, option or exchange real estate. Such activities or processes may include, without limitation, soliciting, advertising, showing or viewing real property, presenting offers or counteroffers, entering into agreements and closing such agreements; and

5. "Firm" means a sole proprietor, corporation, association or partnership.

§59-858-352. Repealed by Laws 2012, c. 251, § 9, eff. Nov. 1, 2013.

§59-858-353. Broker duties and responsibilities.

A. A broker shall have the following duties and responsibilities to all parties in a transaction, which are mandatory and may not be abrogated or waived by a broker:

1. Treat all parties with honesty and exercise reasonable skill and care;

2. Unless specifically waived in writing by a party to the transaction:

a.   receive all written offers and counteroffers,

       b.   reduce offers or counteroffers to a written form upon request of any party to a transaction, and

       c.   present timely all written offers and counteroffers;

3. Timely account for all money and property received by the broker;
4. Keep confidential information received from a party or prospective party confidential. The confidential information shall not be disclosed by a firm without the consent of the party disclosing the information unless consent to the disclosure is granted in writing by the party or prospective party disclosing the information, the disclosure is required by law, or the information is made public or becomes public as the result of actions from a source other than the firm. The following information shall be considered confidential and shall be the only information considered confidential in a transaction:

       a.   that a party or prospective party is willing to pay more or accept less than what is being offered,

       b.   that a party or prospective party is willing to agree to financing terms that are different from those offered,

       c.   the motivating factors of the party or prospective party purchasing, selling, leasing, optioning or exchanging the property, and

       d.   information specifically designated as confidential by a party unless such information is public;

5. Disclose information pertaining to the property as required by the Residential Property Condition Disclosure Act; and
6. Comply with all requirements of The Oklahoma Real Estate License Code and all applicable statutes and rules.

B. A broker shall have the following duties and responsibilities only to a party for whom the broker is providing brokerage services in a transaction which are mandatory and may not be abrogated or waived by a broker:

    1. Inform the party in writing when an offer is made that the party will be expected to pay certain costs, brokerage service costs and approximate amount of the costs; and

    2. Keep the party informed regarding the transaction.

C. When working with both parties to a transaction, the duties and responsibilities set forth in this section shall remain in place for both parties.

§59-858-354. Repealed by Laws 2012, c. 251, § 9, eff. Nov. 1, 2013.

§59-858-355. Repealed by Laws 2012, c. 251, § 9, eff. Nov. 1, 2013.

§59-858-355.1. Brokerage services to both parties in transaction - Disclosure.

A. All brokerage agreements shall incorporate as material terms the duties and responsibilities set forth in Section 858-353 of The Oklahoma Real Estate License Code.

B. A broker may provide brokerage services to one or both parties in a transaction.

C. A broker who is providing brokerage services to one or both parties shall describe and disclose in writing the broker's duties and responsibilities set forth in Section 858-353 of The Oklahoma Real Estate License Code prior to the party or parties signing a contract to sell, purchase, lease, option, or exchange real estate.

D. A firm that provides brokerage services to both parties in a transaction shall provide written notice to both parties that the firm is providing brokerage services to both parties to a transaction prior to the parties signing a contract to purchase, lease, option or exchange real estate.

E. If a broker intends to provide fewer brokerage services than those required to complete a transaction, the broker shall provide written disclosure to the party for whom the broker is providing brokerage services. Such disclosure shall include a description of those steps in the transaction for which the broker will not provide brokerage services, and also state that the broker assisting the other party in the transaction is not required to provide assistance with these steps in any manner.

§59-858-356. Disclosures – Confirmation in writing.

    The written disclosures as required by subsection C of Section 858-355.1 of this title shall be confirmed by each party in writing in a separate provision, incorporated in or attached to the contract to purchase, lease, option, or exchange real estate. In those cases where a broker is involved in a transaction but does not prepare the contract to purchase, lease, option, or exchange real estate, compliance with the disclosure requirements shall be documented by the broker.

§59-858-357. Repealed by Laws 2012, c. 251, § 9, eff. Nov. 1, 2013.

§59-858-358. Duties of broker following termination, expiration or completion of performance.

Except as may be provided in a written brokerage agreement between the broker and a party to a transaction, the broker owes no further duties or responsibilities to the party after termination, expiration, or completion of performance of the transaction, except:

1. To account for all monies and property relating to the transaction; and
2. To keep confidential all confidential information received by the broker during the broker's relationship with a party.

§59-858-359. Payment to broker not determinative of relationship.

A. The payment or promise of payment or compensation by a party to a broker does not determine what relationship, if any, has been established between the broker and a party to a transaction.
B. In the event a broker receives a fee or compensation from any party to the transaction based on a selling price or lease cost of a transaction, such receipt does not constitute a breach of duty or obligation to any party to the transaction.
C. Nothing in this section requires a broker to charge, or prohibits a broker from charging, a separate fee or other compensation for each duty or other brokerage services provided during a transaction.

§59-858-360. Abrogation of common law principles of agency – Remedies cumulative.

A. The duties and responsibilities of a broker specified in Sections 858-351 through 858-363 of The Oklahoma Real Estate License Code shall replace and abrogate the fiduciary or other duties of a broker to a party based on common law principles of agency. The remedies at law and equity supplement the provisions of Sections 858-351 through 858-363 of The Oklahoma Real Estate License Code.
B. A broker may cooperate with other brokers in a transaction. Pursuant to Sections 858-351 through 858-363 of The Oklahoma Real Estate License Code, a broker shall not be an agent, subagent, or dual agent and an offer of subagency shall not be made to other brokers.
C. Nothing in this act shall prohibit a broker from entering into an agreement for brokerage services not enumerated herein so long as the agreement is in compliance with this act, the Oklahoma Real Estate Code and the Oklahoma Real Estate Commission Administration Rules.

§59-858-361. Use of word "agent" in trade name and as general reference.

A real estate broker and the associates of a real estate broker are permitted under the provisions of Sections 858-351 through 858-363 of this title to use the word "agent" in a trade name and as a general reference for designating themselves as real estate licensees.

§59-858-362. Vicarious liability for acts or omissions of real estate licensee.

A party to a real estate transaction shall not be vicariously liable for the acts or omissions of a real estate licensee who is providing brokerage services under Sections 858-351 through 858-363 of The Oklahoma Real Estate License Code.

§59-858-363. Associates of real estate broker - Authority.

Each broker associate, sales associate, and provisional sales associate shall be associated with a real estate broker. Associates shall not enter into a brokerage agreement with a party in the associate's name and shall only be allowed to enter into the agreement in the name of the broker. A real estate broker may authorize associates to provide brokerage services in the name of the real estate broker as permitted under The Oklahoma Real Estate License Code, which may include the execution of written agreements.

§59-858-401. Penalties - Fines - Injunctions and restraining orders - Appeals.

A. In addition to any other penalties provided by law, any person unlicensed pursuant to The Oklahoma Real Estate License Code who shall willingly and knowingly violate any provision of this Code, upon conviction, shall be guilty of a misdemeanor punishable by a fine of not more than One Thousand Dollars ($1,000.00), or by imprisonment in the county jail for not more than six (6) months, or by both such fine and imprisonment.

B. In addition to any civil or criminal actions authorized by law, whenever, in the judgment of the Oklahoma Real Estate Commission, any unlicensed person has engaged in any acts or practices which constitute a violation of the Oklahoma Real Estate License Code, the Commission may:

1. After notice and hearing, and upon finding a violation of the Code, impose a fine of not more than Five Thousand Dollars ($5,000.00) or the amount of the commission or commissions earned, whichever is greater for each violation of the Code for unlicensed activity;

2. Make application to the appropriate court for an order enjoining such acts or practices, and upon a showing by the Commission that such person has engaged in any such acts or practices, an injunction, restraining order, or such other order as may be appropriate shall be granted by such court, without bond; or

3. Impose administrative fines pursuant to this subsection which shall be enforceable in the district courts of this state. The order of the Commission shall become final and binding on all parties unless appealed to the district court as provided in the Administrative Procedures Act. If an appeal is not made, such order may be entered on the judgment docket of the district court in a county in which the debtor has property and thereafter enforced in the same manner as an order of the district court for collection actions.

C. Notices and hearings required by this section and any appeals from orders entered pursuant to this section shall be in accordance with the Administrative Procedures Act.

D. Such funds as collected pursuant to this section shall be deposited in the Oklahoma Real Estate Education and Recovery Fund.

§59-858-402. Administrative fines.

A. The Oklahoma Real Estate Commission may impose administrative fines on any licensee licensed pursuant to The Oklahoma Real Estate License Code as follows:

1. Any administrative fine imposed as a result of a violation of this Code or the rules of the Commission shall not:
   a. be less than One Hundred Dollars ($100.00) and shall not exceed Two Thousand Dollars ($2,000.00) for each violation of this Code or the rules of the Commission, or
   b. exceed Five Thousand Dollars ($5,000.00) for all violations resulting from a single incident or transaction;

2. All administrative fines shall be paid within thirty (30) days of notification of the licensee by the Commission of the order of the Commission imposing the administrative fine;

3. The license may be suspended until any fine imposed upon the licensee by the Commission is paid;

4. If fines are not paid in full by the licensee within thirty (30) days of the notification by the Commission of the order, the fines shall double and the licensee shall have an additional thirty- day period. If the doubled fine is not paid within the additional thirty-day period, the license shall automatically be revoked; and

5. All monies received by the Commission as a result of the imposition of the administrative fine provided for in this section shall be deposited in the Oklahoma Real Estate Education and Recovery Fund, created pursuant to Section 858-601 of this title.

B. The administrative fines authorized by this section may be in addition to any other criminal penalties or civil actions provided for by law.

§59-858-503. Headings.

Article and section headings contained in this Code shall not affect the interpretation of the meaning or intent of any provision of this Code.

§59-858-513. Psychologically impacted real estate - Factors included - Nondisclosure of facts - Certain actions prohibited - Disclosure in certain circumstances.

A. The fact or suspicion that real estate might be or is psychologically impacted, such impact being the result of facts or suspicions, including but not limited to:

1. That an occupant of the real estate is, or was at any time suspected to be infected, or has been infected, with Human Immunodeficiency Virus or diagnosed with Acquired Immune Deficiency Syndrome, or other disease which has been determined by medical evidence to be highly unlikely to be transmitted through the occupancy of a dwelling place; or

2. That the real estate was, or was at any time suspected to have been the site of a suicide, homicide or other felony, is not a material fact that must be disclosed in a real estate transaction.

B. No cause of action shall arise against an owner of real estate or any licensee assisting the owner for the failure to disclose to the purchaser or lessee of such real estate or any licensee assisting the purchaser or lessee that such real estate was psychologically impacted as provided for in subsection A of this section.

C. Notwithstanding the fact that this information is not a material defect or fact, in the event that a purchaser or lessee, who is in the process of making a bona fide offer, advises the licensee assisting the owner, in writing, that knowledge of such factor is important to the person's decision to purchase or lease the property, the licensee shall make inquiry of the owner and report any findings to the purchaser or lessee with the consent of the owner and subject to and consistent with applicable laws of privacy; provided further, if the owner refuses to disclose, the licensee assisting the owner shall so advise the purchaser or lessee.

§59-858-514. Registered sex offenders or violent crime offenders - No duty to provide notice regarding.

The provisions of the Sex Offenders Registration Act and the Mary Rippy Violent Crime Offenders Registration Act shall not be construed as imposing a duty upon a person licensed under the Oklahoma Real Estate License Code to disclose any information regarding an offender required to register under such provision.

§59-858-515.1. Size of property for sale.

A. In connection with any real estate transaction, the size or area, in square footage or otherwise, of the subject property shall not be required to be provided by any real estate licensee, and if provided, shall not be considered any warranty or guarantee of the size or area information, in square footage or otherwise, of the subject property.

B. 1. If a real estate licensee provides any party to a real estate transaction with third-party information concerning the size or area, in square footage or otherwise, of the subject property involved in the transaction, the licensee shall identify the source of the information.

    2. For the purposes of this subsection, "third-party information" means:
  a. an appraisal or any measurement information prepared by a licensed appraiser,
  b. a survey or developer's plan prepared by a licensed surveyor,
  c. a tax assessor's public record,
  d. a builder's plan used to construct or market the property, or
  e. a plan, drawing or stated square footage provided by the owner or agent of the owner, as it relates to commercial buildings or structures for sale or for lease only. Commercial land shall be verified by one of the methods provided for in subparagraphs a through d of this paragraph.

C. A real estate licensee has no duty to the seller or purchaser of real property to conduct an independent investigation of the size or area, in square footage or otherwise, of a subject property, or to independently verify the accuracy of any third-party information as such term is defined in paragraph 2 of subsection B of this section.

D. A real estate licensee who has complied with the requirements of this section, as applicable, shall have no further duties to the seller or purchaser of real property regarding disclosed or undisclosed property size or area information, and shall not be subject to liability to any party for any damages sustained with regard to any conflicting measurements or opinions of size or area, including exemplary or punitive damages.

§59-858-515.2. Violation of duty to disclose source of information - Damages.

A. If a real estate licensee has provided any third-party information, as defined in paragraph 2 of subsection B of Section 1 of this act, to any party to a real estate transaction concerning size or area of the subject real property, a party to the real estate transaction may recover damages from the licensee in a civil action only when a licensee knowingly violates the duty to disclose the source of the information, as required in paragraph 1 of subsection B of Section 1 of this act.

B. The sole and exclusive civil remedy at common law or otherwise for a violation of paragraph 1 of subsection B of Section 1 of this act by a real estate licensee shall be an action for actual damages suffered by the party as a result of such violation and shall not include exemplary or punitive damages.

C. For any real estate transaction commenced after the effective date of this act, any civil action brought pursuant to this section shall be commenced within two (2) years after the date of transfer of the subject real property.

D. In any civil action brought pursuant to this section, the prevailing party shall be allowed court costs and reasonable attorney fees to be set by the court and collected as costs of the action.

E. A transfer of a possessory interest in real property subject to the provisions of this act may not be invalidated solely because of the failure of any person to comply with the provisions of this act.

F. The provisions of this act shall apply to, regulate and determine the rights, duties, obligations and remedies, at common law or otherwise, of the seller marketing his or her real property for sale through a real estate licensee, and of the purchaser of real property offered for sale through a real estate licensee, with respect to disclosure of third-party information concerning the subject real property's size or area, in square footage or otherwise, and this act hereby supplants and abrogates all common law liability, rights, duties, obligations and remedies of all parties therefor.

§59-858-601. Creation - Status - Appropriation - Expenditures - Use of funds - Eligibility to recover.
   A. There is hereby created in the State Treasury a revolving fund for the Oklahoma Real Estate Commission to be designated "Oklahoma Real Estate Education and Recovery Fund". The fund shall consist of monies received by the Oklahoma Real Estate Commission as fees assessed for the Oklahoma Real Estate Education and Recovery Fund under the provisions of this act. The revolving fund shall be a continuing fund not subject to fiscal year limitations and shall be under the administrative direction of the Oklahoma Real Estate Commission. The Oklahoma Real Estate Commission may invest all or part of the monies of the fund in securities offered through the "Oklahoma State Treasurer's Cash Management Program". Any interest or dividends accruing from the securities and any monies generated at the time of redemption of the securities shall be deposited in the Oklahoma Real Estate Education and Recovery Fund. All monies accruing to the credit of the fund are hereby appropriated and may be budgeted and expended by the Oklahoma Real Estate Commission for the purposes specified in Section 858-605 of this title. Expenditures from said fund shall be made pursuant to the laws of this state and the statutes relating to the said Commission, and without legislative appropriation. Warrants for expenditures from said fund shall be drawn by the State Treasurer, based on claims signed by an authorized employee or employees of the said Commission and approved for payment by the Director of the Office of Management and Enterprise Services.
   B. Monies in the fund shall be used to reimburse any claimant who has been awarded a judgment, subject to subsection C of this section, by a court of competent jurisdiction to have suffered monetary damages by an Oklahoma real estate licensee in any transaction for which a license is required under The Oklahoma Real Estate License Code because of an act constituting a violation of The Oklahoma Real Estate License Code.
   C. In determining a claimant's eligibility to recover from the fund, the Commission may conduct an independent review of the merits, findings and damages involved in the underlying action and may conduct an evidentiary hearing to determine if a claim is eligible for recovery from the fund and the amount of damages awarded are due an act constituting a violation of The Oklahoma Real Estate License Code.

§59-858-602. Additional fee - Disposition.
   A. An additional, nonrefundable fee as promulgated by rule by the Commission shall be added to and payable with the license fee for both new licenses and renewals of licenses for each licensee as provided in Section 858-307.1 of this title. Such additional fee shall be deposited in the Oklahoma Real Estate Education and Recovery Fund.
   B. If a license is issued for a period of less than thirty-six (36) months, such additional fee shall be prorated to the nearest dollar and month.
   C. If a real estate sales associate or provisional sales associate shall qualify for a license as a real estate broker, the additional fee for the remainder of the term shall be prorated to the nearest dollar and month and credited to the additional fee added to and payable with the real estate broker license fee.
   D. At the close of each fiscal year, the Commission shall transfer into the Oklahoma Real Estate Commission Revolving Fund any money in excess of that amount required to be retained in the Oklahoma Real Estate Education and Recovery Fund and that amount authorized to be expended as provided within this Code that is remaining in the Oklahoma Education and Recovery Fund and unexpended.

§59-858-603. Eligibility to recover from fund - Ineligibility.
   A. Any claimant shall be eligible to seek recovery from the Oklahoma Real Estate Education and Recovery Fund if the following conditions have been met:
      1. An action has been filed in district court based upon a violation specified in the Oklahoma Real Estate License Code;
      2. The cause of action accrued not more than two (2) years prior to the filing of the action;

3. At the commencement of an action, the party filing the action shall immediately notify the Commission to this effect in writing and provide the Commission with a file-stamped copy of the petition or affidavit. Said Commission shall have the right to enter an appearance, intervene in, defend, or take any action it may deem appropriate to protect the integrity of the Fund. The Commission may waive the notification requirement if it determines that the public interest is best served by the waiver, that is to best meet the ends of justice and that the claimant making application made a good faith effort to comply with the notification requirements;

4. Final judgment is received by the claimant upon such action;

5. The final judgment is enforced as provided by statute for enforcement of judgments in other civil actions and that the amount realized was insufficient to satisfy the judgment; and

6. Any compensation recovered by the claimant from the judgment debtor, or from any other source for any monetary loss arising out of the cause of action, has been applied to the judgment awarded by the court.

B. A claimant shall not be qualified to make a claim for recovery from the Oklahoma Real Estate Education and Recovery Fund, if:

1. The claimant is the spouse of the judgment debtor or a personal representative of such spouse;

2. The claimant is a licensee who acted in their own behalf in the transaction which is the subject of the claim; or

3. The claimant's claim is based upon a real estate transaction in which the claimant is, through their own action, jointly responsible for any resulting monetary loss with respect to the property owned or controlled by the claimant.

§59-858-604. Application for payment - Amount - Assignment of rights, etc. - Insufficient funds - Revocation of licenses.

A. Any claimant who meets all of the conditions prescribed by this act may apply to the Commission for payment from the Oklahoma Real Estate Education and Recovery Fund, in an amount equal to the unsatisfied portion of the claimant's judgment, which is actual or compensatory damages, or Twenty-five Thousand Dollars ($25,000.00), whichever is less. The claimant is entitled to reimbursement for attorney fees reasonably incurred in the litigation not to exceed twenty-five percent (25%) of the claimant's amount approved by the Commission. Attorney fees charged and received shall be documented, verified, and submitted with the claim. Court costs and other expenses shall not be recoverable from the fund.

B. Upon receipt by the claimant of the payment from the Oklahoma Real Estate Education and Recovery Fund, the claimant assigns the claimant's right, title and interest in that portion of the judgment to the Commission which shall be subrogated up to the amount actually paid by the fund to the claimant or to the claimant and the claimant's attorney. Upon suit to collect upon a judgment, the claimant shall have priority over the fund. Any amount subsequently recovered on the judgment by the Commission, to the extent of the Commission's right, title and interest therein, shall be used to reimburse the Oklahoma Real Estate Education and Recovery Fund.

C. Payments for claims arising out of the same transaction which constitutes a claimant's cause of action based upon a violation of the Oklahoma Real Estate License Code shall be limited in the aggregate of Fifty Thousand Dollars ($50,000.00) irrespective of the number of claimants or parcels of real estate involved in the transaction.

D. Payments for claims based upon judgments against any one licensee shall not exceed in the aggregate Fifty Thousand Dollars ($50,000.00).

E. If at any time the monies in the Oklahoma Real Estate Education and Recovery Fund are insufficient to satisfy any valid claim, or portion thereof, the Commission shall satisfy such unpaid claim or portion thereof as soon as a sufficient amount of money has been deposited in the fund by collecting a special levy from members of the fund of an amount not to exceed Five Dollars ($5.00) each fiscal year. If the additional levy is not sufficient to pay all outstanding claims against the fund, the claims shall be paid as the money becomes available. Where there is more than one claim outstanding, the claims shall be paid in the order that they were approved.

F. Any claim against a corporation, association or partnership would be imputed to the managing broker(s) at the time the cause of action arose.

G. The license of said licensee shall be automatically revoked upon the payment of any amount from the Oklahoma Real Estate Education and Recovery Fund on a judgment against a licensee. The license shall not be considered for reinstatement until the licensee has repaid in full, plus interest at the rate of seven percent (7%) a year, the amount paid from the Oklahoma Real Estate Education and Recovery Fund on the judgment against the licensee.

§59-858-605. Expenditure of funds.

At any time when the total amount of monies deposited in the Oklahoma Real Estate Education and Recovery Fund exceeds Two Hundred Fifty Thousand Dollars ($250,000.00), the Commission in its discretion may expend such excess funds each fiscal year for the following purposes:

1. To promote the advancement of education in the field of real estate for the benefit of the general public and those licensed under the Oklahoma Real Estate License Code, but such promotion shall not be construed to allow advertising of this profession;

2. To underwrite educational seminars and other forms of educational projects for the benefit of real estate licensees;

3. To establish real estate courses at institutions of higher learning located in the state and accredited by the State Regents for Higher Education for the purpose of making such courses available to licensees and the general public; and

4. To contract for a particular educational project in the field of real estate to further the purposes of the Oklahoma Real Estate License Code.

Oklahoma Real Estate Commission Rules

Title 605 - Oklahoma Real Estate Commission

Chapter 1 - Administrative Operations

Subchapter 1 – General Provisions

605:1-1-1. Statement of purpose

The fundamental and primary purpose of the Real Estate Commission is to safeguard public interest and provide quality services by assisting and providing resources; encouraging and requiring high standards of knowledge and ethical practices of licensees; investigating and sanctioning licensed activities; and through the prosecution of any unlicensed person who violates the "Oklahoma Real Estate License Code and Rules."

605:1-1-2. Authority

The rules of this Title are hereby adopted in accordance with the provisions of Title 59, Section 858-101 et seq. and the provisions of Sections 301-327 of Title 75, Oklahoma Statutes, 1971.

605:1-1-3. Title and construction

The rules of this Title shall be known as the "Oklahoma Real Estate Commission Rules."

605:1-1-4. Operational procedures

(a) **Organization.** The organization of the Commission is declared to be that as enumerated in Sections 858-201 through 858-204 of the heretofore described Code.

(b) **Operational procedures.** The general course and method of operation shall be as hereinafter specified in overall provisions of the rules of this Title.

(c) **Open Records Act.** In conformance with Title 51, Section 24 A.1., et seq, Oklahoma Statutes, 1985, titled "Oklahoma Open Records Act" all open records of the Real Estate Commission may be inspected and copied in accordance with procedures, policies, and fee as required by the Commission. The Commission shall charge the following:

    (1) A fee of $.25 for each xerographic copy or micrographic image.

    (2) A fee of $1.00 for each copy to be certified.

    (3) A fee of $10.00 per hour for a record or file search.

    (4) A fee of Forty Dollars ($40.00) per extract for License Data extract.

    (5) A fee of Fifty Dollars ($50.00) every three (3) months for an Examinee Data extract.

    (6) A fee of no more than Seven Dollars and Fifty Cents ($7.50) for a convenience fee for any electronic/on-line transaction.

(d) **Petition for promulgation, amendment or repeal of any rule.** Any person may petition the Commission in writing requesting a promulgation, amendment or repeal of any rule.

    (1) The petition must be in writing in business letter form or in the form of petitions used in civil cases in this State, and shall contain an explanation and the implications of the request and shall be:

        (A) Signed by the person filing the petition and be filed with the Secretary-Treasurer of the Commission.

        (B) Submitted to the Commission at least thirty (30) days prior to a regular meeting.

        (C) Considered by the Commission at its first meeting following such thirty (30) days.

        (D) Scheduled for a public hearing before the Commission within sixty (60) days after being considered by the Commission in a regular meeting.

    (2) Within sixty (60) days after the public hearing, the Commission shall either grant or deny the petition. If the petition is granted, the Commission shall immediately begin the procedure for the promulgation, amendment or repeal of any rule pursuant to Title 75 O.S. 303.

    (3) If the petition is denied the parties retain their rights under 75 O.S. Sec. 318, to proper Judicial Review.

(e) **Petition for declaratory ruling of any rule or order.**

(1) Any person may petition the Commission for a declaratory ruling as authorized by Section 307 of Title 75 of the Oklahoma Statutes as to the applicability of any rule or order of the Commission. Such petition shall:

(A) be in writing;

(B) be signed by the person seeking the ruling;

(C) state the rule or order involved;

(D) contain a brief statement of facts to which the ruling shall apply; and

(E) if known and available to petitioner, include citations of legal authority in support of such views.

(2) The Commission shall have at least thirty (30) days to review the petition. Following the review period, the Commission shall consider the petition at its next meeting.

(3) The Commission may compel the production of testimony and evidence necessary to make its declaratory ruling.

(4) Declaratory rulings shall be available for review by the public at the Commission office.

(f) **Contract Forms Committee.**

(1) The contract forms committee is required to draft and revise real estate purchase and/or lease contracts and any related addenda for standardization and use by real estate licensees (Title 59 O.S. 858-208 (14).

(2) The committee shall consist of eleven (11) members. Three (3) members shall be appointed by the Oklahoma Real Estate Commission; three (3) members shall be appointed by the Oklahoma Bar Association; and five (5) members shall be appointed by the Oklahoma Association of Realtors, Incorporated.

(3) The initial members' terms shall begin upon development of the forms and each member shall serve through the effective date of implementation of form(s) plus one (1) year. Thereafter, the Oklahoma Real Estate Commission shall appoint one (1) member for one (1) year, one (1) member for two (2) years, and one (1) member for three (3) years; the Oklahoma Bar Association shall appoint one (1) member for one (1) year, one (1) member for two (2) years, and one (1) member for three (3) years and; the Oklahoma Association of Realtors, Incorporated shall appoint two (2) members for one (1) year, two (2) members for two (2) years, and one (1) member for three (3) years. Thereafter, terms shall be for three (3) years and each member shall serve until their term expires and their successor has been appointed. Any vacancy which may occur in the membership of the committee shall be filled by the appropriate appointing entity.

(4) A member can be removed for just cause by the committee.

(5) Each member of the committee shall be entitled to receive travel expenses essential to the performance of the duties of his appointment, as provided in the State Travel Reimbursement Act.

(g) Oklahoma Education and Recovery Fund. If a special levy is assessed on licensees as outlined in Title 59 O.S. 858-604 (E), the levy must be paid within sixty (60) days of assessment or the license will be placed on inactive status and shall not be placed on active status until the levy is paid.

Title 605 - Oklahoma Real Estate Commission

Chapter 10 - Requirements, Standards and Procedures

Subchapter 1 – General Provisions
Subchapter 3 – Education and Examination Requirements
Subchapter 5 – Education and Examination Requirements
Subchapter 7 – Licensing Procedures and Options
Subchapter 9 – Broker's Operational Procedures
Subchapter 11 – Associate's Licensing Procedures
Subchapter 13 – Trust Account Procedures
Subchapter 15 – Disclosures, Brokerage Services and Statute of Frauds
Subchapter 17 – Causes for Investigation; Hearing Process; Prohibited Acts; Discipline

Appendix A – Residential Property Disclosure Statement
Appendix B – Residential Property Condition Disclaimer Statement Form

605:10-1-1. Purpose

Oklahoma Real Estate Commission Rules

The rules of this Chapter establish procedures and standards that apply to real estate licensees, real estate schools and instructors, and which must be complied with as authorized under the provisions of the Oklahoma Real Estate License Code, Title 59, O.S., Sections 858-101 through 858-605.

605:10-1-2. Definitions

When used in this Chapter, masculine words shall include the feminine and neuter, and the singular includes the plural. The following words or terms, when used in this Chapter, shall have the following meaning, unless the context clearly indicates otherwise:

"Advertising" means all forms of representation, promotion and solicitation disseminated in any manner and by any means of communication, to include social networking, to consumers for any purpose related to licensed real estate activity.

"Bona fide offer" means an offer in writing.

"Branch office" means an extension of a broker's main office location and normally is located at a different location than the main office. A branch office shall not be independently owned by any person other than the applicable broker or entity.

"Branch office broker" means a person who qualified for a broker license and who is designated by a broker manager or proprietor broker to direct and supervise a branch office on behalf of the broker in conformance with Section 858-310 of the Code. A branch office broker is considered an associate of the a broker manager or proprietor broker.

"Broker" means a sole proprietor, corporation, managing corporate broker of a corporation, association, managing broker member or manager of an association, partnership, or managing partners of a partnership and shall be one and the same as defined as a broker in Section 858-102 of the Code and whom the Commission shall hold responsible for all actions of associates who are assigned to said broker.

"Code" when used in the rules of this Chapter, means Title 59, Section 858-101 et seq, Oklahoma Statutes as adopted 1974 and amended.

"Entity" means association, corporation and partnership.

"Filed" means the date of the United States postal service postmark or the date personal delivery is made to the Commission office.

"Firm" means a sole proprietor, corporation, association or partnership.

"Inactive status" means a period in which a licensee is prohibited from performing activities which require an active license.

"Nonresident" means a person who is licensed to practice in this state, however, does not maintain a place of business in this state but maintains a place of business in another state and who periodically comes to this state to operate and perform real estate activities.

"Previously licensed applicant" means a person who has been licensed in another state and desires to obtain a resident license in this state.

"Provisional sales associate" shall be synonymous in meaning with sales associate except where it is specifically addressed in Subchapters 3, 5 and 7 of this Chapter.

"Rents or leases real estate" as referenced in Title 59, Section 858-101, subparagraph 2, means the licensed activities provided by a broker through a property management agreement with a party for a fee, commission or other valuable consideration, or with the intention or expectation of receiving or collecting a fee, commission or other valuable consideration. Licensed property management activities may include, but shall not be limited to, showing real property for rent or lease; soliciting tenants and landlords; negotiating on behalf of the tenant or landlord; and complying with and maintaining the property in accordance with Title 41, Oklahoma Statutes, Non-Residential/Residential Landlord and Tenant Acts.

"Resident" means a person who is licensed in this state and operates from a place of business in this state.

"Sole proprietor" means a broker who is the sole owner of a real estate business.

"Team name" means a name used by a team as defined in Section 858-305 of the Code. All team names must be approved by the broker and must be registered with the Commission.

"Trade name" means the name a firm is to be known as and which is used in advertising by the firm to promote and generate publicity for the firm. A firm may or may not do business in the name under which their license is issued but must register with the Commission all trade names used by the firm.

605:10-1-3. Appeal of administrative decisions; procedures

(a) Unless specifically provided for elsewhere in this Chapter, any adverse administrative action or decision rendered by the Commission, its staff on behalf of the Commissionor a third party contract vendor, may be appealed by the adversely affected party filing within thirty (30) days of notice of such action or decision, a written request for a hearing.

(b) Upon receipt of a request for any non-disciplinary hearing provided for in this Section, or any other rule of this Chapter, the Secretary-Treasurer shall schedule an administrative decision hearing before a Hearing Examiner, a selected panel of the Commission, or the Commission as a whole giving at least fifteen (15) days notice of such hearing. Such hearing shall be public except that upon motion, witnesses, other than the adversely affected appealing party, may be excluded from the hearing room when such witnesses are not testifying. A court reporter shall be present to record the proceedings in behalf of the Commission. Any person desiring a copy of the transcript of the proceedings may purchase such from the reporter.

(c) In the case of a proceeding conducted by the Commission as a whole or a panel of the Commission, the Chairman or his designee shall preside. Designated counsel shall advise the chair as to rulings upon the questions of admissibility of evidence, competence of witnesses and any other question of law where such ruling is required or requested.

(d) The appealing party may present his or her own evidence or may present such through his or her counsel. In order that the hearing will not be encumbered by evidence having no bearing on the issues, testimony by all witnesses will be limited to matters relevant to the issues involved.

(e) The order of procedure shall be as follows:
  (1) Recitation of the administrative action or decision.
  (2) Presentation of the adversely affected party's appeal.
  (3) Questioning of the appealing party by the hearing panel or Hearing Examiner.
  (4) Response by the Commission or Commission representatives detailing grounds for and basis for the administrative decision or action.
  (5) Examination of witnesses by appealing party with cross-examination of such witnesses.
  (6) Closing statements by the appealing party.

(f) If the case is heard by the Commission as a whole, the Commission shall deliberate and render its decision with confirmation of such decision in writing in the form of an Order distributed to all parties by mail.

(g) In the case of a hearing conducted by a Hearing Examiner or a panel of the Commission, following the hearing, the Hearing Examiner or attorney sitting as counsel to the panel of the Commission shall prepare a recommended Order to be considered by the Real Estate Commission as a whole at a future meeting. All parties will be furnished copies of the recommended Order and notified as to the date the recommendations will be considered by the Commission for adoption. At the same time, notice will be given also to the parties that written exceptions or requests to present oral exceptions or arguments, if any, should be submitted on or before a designated date pursuant to Section 311, Title 75, Oklahoma Statutes. Upon adoption of the recommended Order by the Commission as a whole, such Order shall be distributed to all parties.

605:10-1-4. Returned checks - disposition

(a) All fees are received subject to collection. Payment of a fee to the Commission with a dishonored check may be prima facie evidence of a violation of Title 59, Section 858-312.

(b) If the Commission receives a check that is dishonored upon presentation to the bank on which the check is drawn, a returned check fee of Thirty-five Dollars ($35.00) will be charged. If such payment is for fees, or other amounts due the Commission, and the check is not replaced within the specified time frame as determined by the Commission, such request shall be deemed incomplete and the transaction null and void.

(c) Other services may be delayed or denied if a check is dishonored upon presentation to the bank on which the check is drawn.

605:10-3-1. Prelicense education requirements

(a) On and after July 1, 1993, as evidence of an applicant's having satisfactorily completed those education requirements as set forth in Sections 858-302 and 858-303 of the Code, each applicant for licensure shall present with his or her application a certification showing successful completion of the applicable course of study approved by the Commission as follows:
  (1) To qualify an applicant for examination and licensure as a provisional sales associate, the course shall consist of at least ninety (90) clock hours of instruction or its equivalent as determined by the Commission. In order for a provisional sales associate to obtain a sales associate license, the provisional sales associate must, following issuance of a provisional license, complete additional education as required in Section 858-302 of the Code. The prelicense course of study shall be referred to as the Basic Course of Real Estate, Part I of II and shall encompass the following areas of study:
  (A) Real Estate Economics and Marketing

    (B) Nature of Real Estate

    (C) Rights and Interest in Real Estate

    (D) Legal Descriptions

    (E) Title Search, Encumbrances, and Land Use Control

    (F) Transfer of Rights

    (G) Service Contracts

    (H) Estimating Transaction Expenses

    (I) Value and Appraisal

    (J) Marketing Activities

    (K) Fair Housing

    (L) Contract Law Overview

    (M) Contract Law and Performance

    (N) Offers and Purchase Contracts

    (O) Financing Real Estate

    (P) Closing a Transaction

    (Q) Regulations Affecting Real Estate

    (R) Disclosures and Environmental Issues

    (S) Property Management and Leasing

    (T) Risk Management

    (U) Professional Standards of Conduct

    (V) Law of Agency

(2) To qualify an applicant for examination and licensure as a broker or a broker associate, the course shall consist of at least ninety (90) clock hours of instruction or its equivalent as determined by the Commission. Such course of study shall be referred to as the Advanced Course in Real Estate and shall encompass the following areas of study:

    (A) Laws and Rules Affecting Real Estate Practice

    (B) Broker Supervision

    (C) Establishing a Real Estate Office

    (D) Professional Development

    (E) Business, Financial, and Brokerage Management

    (F) Oklahoma Broker Relationships

    (G) Anti-Trust and Deceptive Trade

    (H) Risk Management and Insurance

    (I) Mandated Disclosures, Hazards, and Zoning

    (J) Real Estate Financing

    (K) Specialized Property Operations and Specialty Areas

    (L) Trust Accounts and Trust Funds

    (M) Closing a Real Estate Transaction

    (N) Closing Statements

    (O) Professional Standards of Conduct

    (P) Property Ownership

    (Q) Land Use Controls and Regulations

    (R) Valuation and Market Analysis

    (S) Law of Agency

    (T) Contracts

    (U) Transfer of Property

    (V) Practice of Real Estate

    (W) Real Estate Calculations

(b) As evidence of an applicant's having successfully completed those education requirements as set forth in Section 858-304 of the Code, each applicant shall present a certified transcript from an institution of higher education, accredited by the Oklahoma State Regents for Higher Education or the corresponding accrediting agency of another jurisdiction.

    (1) The basic course of real estate shall be limited to Basic Real Estate Principles and Practices; provided, however, that a course or combination of courses not so titled may be accepted if the course content has been determined by the Commission to be equivalent as one and the same as enumerated in this Section.

(2) The advanced course of real estate shall be limited to Advanced Real Estate Principles and Practices; provided that a course or combination of courses not so titled may be accepted if the course content has been determined by the Commission to be equivalent as one and the same as that enumerated in this Section.

(3) The Commission shall accept in lieu of a certified transcript a course completion certificate as prescribed by the Commission.

(c) **Entities allowed to seek approval.** The education courses required of this Section shall be satisfied by courses approved by the Commission and offered by:

(1) The Commission

(2) An area vocational-technical school

(3) A college or university

(4) A private school

(5) The Oklahoma Association of Realtors, the National Association of Realtors, or any affiliate thereof,

(6) The Oklahoma Bar Association, American Bar Association, or any affiliate thereof; or

(7) An education provider.

(d) **Attendance and successful completion required for in-class credit.** To complete any in-class offering, a person must physically be present during all of the offering time and successfully complete all course requirements to include an examination.

(e) **Successful completion of materials and examination required for distance education credit.** To complete a distance education course offering, a person must successfully complete all course requirements to include all modules and an examination.

605:10-3-2. Application for license

(a) **Requirements for completing application.**

(1) Any person seeking a real estate license shall make application for such license on a form provided by the Commission. The form shall contain, but not be limited to, the following:

(A) Legal name to include first, middle and last name.

(B) Routine biographical information.

(C) License history in Oklahoma and other states.

(D) Criminal and/or civil charges or convictions, including bankruptcy and judgments.

(E) Compliance with Title 59 O.S. 858.301.1 regarding felony convictions.

(F) Recent photograph.

(G) Birth date.

(H) Evidence of successful completion of course requirement as specified in the "Code".

(I) If applicable, evidence of transaction experience as specified in the "Code."

(J) If applicable, evidence of successful completion of the Broker in Charge course.

(K) A sworn statement as to accuracy of the application information.

(L) Documentation required for compliance necessary to verify citizenship, qualified alien status, and eligibility under the Personal Responsibility and Work Opportunity Reconciliation Act of 1996.

(M) Social security number, pursuant to Title 56, Oklahoma Statutes, Section 240.21A.

(N) Submit to a national criminal history record check, as defined by Section 150.9 of Title 74 of the Oklahoma Statutes. A fee amount, not to exceed sixty dollars ($60.00), shall be sent to the Commission to begin the process of the national criminal history check.

(O) A completed national criminal history record check, completed for the Commission, shall be valid for six (6) months from the date of issuance from the issuing authority.

(P) In the event an applicant is not physically able to submit to finger printing, other applicant identifiers shall be utilized, i.e., name, birth date and social security number.

(2) An applicant indicating a bankruptcy or judgment, criminal and/or civil charges or convictions on the application, must submit with the application official documents to the Commission which pertain to the disposition of the matter. If official documents are unable to be obtained, a detailed letter explaining the matter(s) must be attached to the application.

(b) **Applicant shall appear for examination.** Each applicant shall appear for an examination as soon as possible subsequent to the filing of an approved application or the signing of a form as required in 605:10-3-3.

(c) **Applicant must be of good moral character.** The application submitted by an individual seeking a license must indicate that the applicant possesses a reputation for honesty, truthfulness, trustworthiness, good moral character, and that he or she bears a good reputation for fair dealing.

(d) **Determining good moral character.** In determining whether or not an applicant meets the definition of good moral character, the Commission will consider, but not be limited to, the following:

(1) Whether the probation period given in a conviction or deferred sentence has been completed and fully satisfied to include fines, court costs, etc.

(2) Whether the restitution ordered by a court in a criminal conviction or civil judgement has been fully satisfied.

(3) Whether a bankruptcy that is real estate related has been discharged.

(4) Whether an applicant has been denied licensure or a license has been suspended or revoked by this or any other state or jurisdiction to practice or conduct any regulated profession, business or vocation because of any conduct or practices which would have warranted a like result under the Oklahoma "Code".

(5) Whether an applicant has been guilty of conduct or practices in this state or elsewhere which would have been grounds for revocation or suspension under the current Oklahoma "Code" had the applicant been licensed.

(e) **Subsequent good conduct.** If, because of lapse of time and subsequent good conduct and reputation or other reason deemed sufficient, it shall appear to the Commission that the interest of the public will not likely be in danger by the granting of such license, the Commission may approve the applicant as relates to good moral character.

605:10-3-3. Proceedings upon application for a license

(a) **Qualified application.**

(1) **Approved application.** If the Commission is of the opinion that an applicant for license is qualified, the application shall be approved. An approved application shall be valid for ninety (90) days.

(2) **Denial of application.** If, from the application filed, or from answers to inquiries, or from complaints or information received, or from investigation, it shall appear to the Commission the applicant is not qualified at any time before the initial license is issued, the Commission shall refuse to approve the application and shall give notice of that fact to the applicant within fifteen (15) days after its ruling, order or decision.

(b) **Appeal of denial of application.** Upon written request from the applicant, filed within thirty (30) days after receipt of such notice of denial, the Commission shall set the matter for hearing to be conducted within sixty (60) days after receipt of the applicant's request.

(c) **Applicant hearing.** The hearing shall be at the time and place as prescribed by the Commission. At least ten (10) days prior to the date set for hearing the Commission shall notify the applicant and other persons protesting, and shall set forth in a notice the reason or reasons why the Commission refused to accept or approve the application. The written notice of the hearing may be served by personal delivery to the applicant and protesters, or by mailing the same by registered or certified mail to the last known address of the applicant and/or protesters.

(d) **Hearing procedures.** The hearing procedure shall be that as outlined in 605:10-1-3 titled "Appeal of administrative decisions; procedures."

605:10-3-4. Broker applicant; experience

(a) No individual shall be licensed as a real estate broker unless in addition to the other requirements in the Code, he or she has served two (2) years, or its equivalent, as a licensed real estate sales associate and/or broker associate, with and under the instructions and guidance of a licensed real estate broker of this state or any other state at least twenty-four (24) months within the five (5) year period immediately prior to the filing of his or her application for license as a real estate broker in Oklahoma. Additionally, no individual shall be licensed as a real estate broker unless he or she can provide documentation verifying ten real estate transactions as defined in Section 858-351 of the Code within the past five years, or the equivalent thereof, as determined by the Commission. Such documentation shall be demonstrated on forms developed by the Commission.

(b) An application submitted for the purpose of seeking a license to function as a real estate broker shall not be accepted for filing by the Commission unless such applicant has completed the two (2) year licensure requirement on or before the date such application is submitted.

605.10-3-4.1. Broker associate applicant; experience

(a) No individual shall be licensed as a real estate broker associate unless in addition to the other requirements in the Code, he or she has served two years, or its equivalent, as a licensed real estate provisional sales associate and/or sales associate, with and under the instructions and guidance of a licensed real estate broker of this state or any other state at least twenty-four (24) months within the five(5) year period immediately prior to the filing of hisor her application for license as a real estate broker associate in Oklahoma.

(b) An application submitted for the purpose of seeking a license to function as a real estate broker associate shall not be accepted for filing by the Commission until such applicant has completed the two (2) year licensure requirement on or before the date such application is submitted.

605:10-3-5. Examinations

(a) **Applicant must appear in person.** When an application for examination has been submitted to the Commission, the applicant shall be required to appear in person, at a time and place to be designated by the Commission, and answer questions based on the required subject matter as prescribed elsewhere in the rules of this Chapter. On and after August 1, 2001, each broker examination fee shall be Seventy-five Dollars ($75.00) and each provisional sales associate/sales associate examination fee shall be Sixty Dollars ($60.00.)

(b) **Special accommodations.** In cases where special accommodations are necessary under the requirements of the Americans with Disabilities Act, applicants must notify the examination supplier in advance by submitting a written request, on a form prescribed by the Commission, describing the disability and necessary accommodations.

(c) **Failure to pass examination.** If an applicant fails to pass the examination prescribed by the Commission, the Commission may permit subsequent examinations upon receipt of a new examination fee for each examination to be attempted.

(d) **Applicant request to view failed examination.** An applicant who fails the examination has the option of reviewing their missed questions at the end of their examination. An applicant may challenge the validity of any question(s) they identify as incorrectly graded. A challenge to a question that pertains to the Oklahoma law portion of the examination will be sent to the Commission by the examination supplier. A challenge to a question that pertains to the national portion will fall under the review policy of the examination supplier. In either case, both the examination supplier and/or the Commission shall have five (5) business days in which to review and issue a response to the applicant. Applicants will be allowed up to one (1) hour to review their exam and the applicant will not be allowed to test on the same day they review a failed examination. No notes, pencils or electronic devices will be allowed during review nor will they be allowed to leave the examination area with the examination questions.

(e) **Application valid for one year.** The original examination application shall be valid for one (1) year from date of filing. After such date, an applicant must complete a new original application form.

(f) **Passing percentile of examination.** A score of seventy-five percent (75%) or more shall be considered a passing grade on the broker or provisional sales associate/sales associate examination.

(g) **Validity period of examination results.** The results of an examination wherein an applicant scored a passing grade shall be valid for one (1) year from the date of such examination.

(h) **Disciplinary examination fee.** A fee shall be charged for an examination which is directed by Order of the Commission as disciplinary action.

(i) **Examination voided.** A licensee or instructor applicant caught cheating during the course of a real estate examination shall:
   (1) immediately forfeit the examination,
   (2) be given a failing score,
   (3) be disqualified from retaking the examination for one year, and
   (4) be allowed to file an appeal with the Commission under Rule 605:10-1-3.

605:10-3-6. Continuing education requirements

(a) **Definition.** Continuing education shall be defined as any real estate oriented education course or equivalent, hereinafter called offering(s) intended:
   (1) To improve the knowledge of licensees.
   (2) To keep licensees abreast of changing real estate practices and laws.
   (3) To help licensees meet the statutory requirements for license renewal.

(b) **Purpose.** The purpose of continuing education is to provide an educational program through which real estate licensees can continually become more competent and remain qualified to engage in real estate activities for which they are licensed. Such activities involve facts and concepts about which licensees must be knowledgeable in order to safely and confidently conduct real estate negotiations and transactions in the public's best interest.

(c) **Goals.** The goals of continuing education are:

    (1) To provide licensees with opportunity for obtaining necessary current information and knowledge which will enable them to conduct real estate negotiations and transactions in a legal and professional manner in order to better protect public interest.

    (2) To assure that the licensees are provided with current information regarding new and/or changing laws and regulations which affect the real estate business.

    (3) To ensure that the consumers interest is protected from unknowledgeable licensees.

(d) **Objectives.** The objectives of continued education are as follows:

    (1) For licensees to expand and enhance their knowledge and expertise so as to be continually effective, competent, and ethical as they practice real estate.

    (2) For licensees to review and update their knowledge of federal, state and local laws and regulations which affect real estate practices.

(e) **Entities allowed to seek approval.** The Commission may approve and/or accept any offering provided by an entity which meets the purposes, goals, and objectives of the continuing education requirement. The Commission may accept the following offerings as proof of meeting the continuing education requirement:

    (1) Any offering which is approved and presented by those entities enumerated in paragraph B, of 858- 307.2 of the "Code".

    (2) Any offering in real estate, or directly related area, approved and/or accepted by the real estate regulatory agency in another state; provided such offering is not excluded elsewhere in this Chapter.

    (3) Any offering in real estate, or directly related area, not accepted in paragraphs (1) or (2) of this subsection, which can be determined by the Commission to be in compliance with the intent of the rules of this Chapter.

    (4) Completion of an approved ninety (90) hour prelicense broker course or an approved forty-five (45) hour provisional sales associate postlicense course, or its respective equivalent as determined by the Commission shall suffice for 21-hours of continuing education credit for a licensee. An individual segment of an approved prelicense broker course or an approved provisional sales associate postlicense course shall suffice for continuing education credit provided such individual segment has also been separately approved for continuing education credit.

(f) **Ineligible courses.**

    (1) The following offerings will not be considered by the Commission to meet continuing education requirements:

        (A) General training or education not directly related to real estate or real estate practices.

        (B) Offerings in mechanical office and business skills such as typing, speed reading, memory improvement, report writing, and personal motivation that is not directly related to real estate.

        (C) Sales promotion or other meetings held in conjunction with the general real estate brokerage business.

        (D) Meetings which are a normal part of in-house training.

        (E) That portion of any offering devoted to breakfast, luncheon, dinner, or other refreshments.

        (F) Prelicense general training and education to obtain a provisional sales associate or sales associate license or license examination refresher courses for provisional sales associate/sales associate or broker.

    (2) The list in (1) of this subsection does not limit the Commission's authority to disapprove any offering which fails to meet the adopted purposes, goals and objectives.

(g) **List of approved entities.** The Commission shall maintain a list of approved entities.

(h) **Licensee responsible for notification to Commission.** Each licensee shall be ultimately responsible to the Commission to furnish evidence of having successfully completed the continuing education requirements for license renewal, activation, or reinstatement, as set forth elsewhere in this Chapter. Each licensee shall present to the Commission evidence of completion of a minimum of twenty-one (21) clock hours of continuing education offerings acceptable by the Commission. As evidence of having completed the requirement each licensee shall present:

    (1) A certificate, and/or documents, statements and forms, as may reasonably be required by the Commission, or

    (2) A certified transcript; provided, however, if such offering is taken as an accredited C.E.U. (Continuing Education Unit) a certificate may be accepted in lieu of the transcript.

(i) **Attendance and successful completion required for in-class credit.** To complete any in-class offering, a person must physically be present during all of the offering time and successfully complete all course requirements.

(j) **Successful completion of materials and examination required for distance education credit.** To complete a distance education course offering, a person must successfully complete all course requirements to include all modules and an examination.

(k) **Course limitations.**

    (1) A particular course offering may not be taken for continuing education credit more than once from the same entity and/or instructor during a renewal period.

    (2) Educational courses taken for disciplinary reasons shall not count towards the normal continuing education requirements for licensees.

(l) **Required number of continuing education hours.** The required number of continuing education hours for a licensee shall be as follows:

    (1) As a condition of a license activation or active reinstatement, each license with an expiration date of June 30, 2014 and thereafter, with the exception of those exempt as set out in Title 59, 858-307.2, shall provide evidence of completion of twenty-one (21) clock hours of Commission approved subject matter, or its equivalent, as determined by the Commission. Such hours shall have been taken in the same license term for which the license is to be issued, with the exception of a licensee whose hours were not used in the preceding license term. In that case, the hours taken in the preceding license term shall count towards an applicable license activation or active reinstatement.

    (2) Each licensee shall have completed of said twenty-one (21) clock hours of continuing education six (6) clock hours of required subject matter as directed by the Commission.

    (3) The required subject matter, or its equivalent, as determined by the Commission, shall consist of at least one (1) clock hour in all following subjects each license term: Professional Conduct, Broker Relationships Act, Fair Housing, Contracts and Forms, Code and Rule Updates and Current Issues. The remaining fifteen (15) clock hours may consist of elective subject matter as approved by the Commission.

    (4) Any licensee may complete the Broker in Charge course as approved by the Commission consisting of fifteen (15) clock hours in lieu of the required subject matter.

    (5) All Broker shall be required to successfully complete the Broker in Charge course as approved by the Commission consisting of fifteen (15) clock hours, or its equivalent, as approved by the Commission. In addition, to complete the continuing education requirement of twenty-one (21) clock hours such broker shall complete at least two (2) of the six (6) required subject matter, equal to at least six (6) clock hours, as referenced in paragraph (3) of this subsection.

    (6) Any broker that lapsed or renewed inactive in their previous license term or current license term who applies for reinstatement or activation must complete the Broker in Charge course and two (2) of the six (6) required subject matter equal to at least six (6) hours prior to their license being reinstated active or reactivating.

605:10-3-7. Provisional sales associate post-license education requirement

(a) **Purpose.** The purpose of the provisional sales associate post-license education requirement is to provide an educational program through which real estate provisional sales associate licensees can become more competent, knowledgeable and perfect their ability to engage in real estate activities for which they are licensed. Such activities involve facts and concepts which licensees must be knowledgeable in order to safely and confidently conduct real estate negotiations and transactions in the public's best interest.

(b) **Goals.** The goals of the provisional sales associate post-license education requirements are:

    (1) To provide newly licensed individuals with the opportunity to obtain current information and knowledge to enable them to conduct real estate negotiations and transactions in a legal and professional manner in order to better protect public interest.

    (2) To assure that licensees are provided with relevant information pertaining to practices which directly relate to real estate business.

    (3) To assure that the provisional sales associate is provided with information regarding new and/or changing laws and regulations which affect the real estate business.

    (4) To assure that the consumers interest is protected from unknowledgeable licensees.

(c) **Objectives.** The objectives of post-license education are to:

    (1) Assist newly licensed individuals by having available a practical educational program wherein the information attained can be put into practice.

    (2) To help licensees expand and enhance their knowledge and expertise so as to continually be effective, competent, and ethical as they practice real estate.

(3) To encourage licensees to gain additional education for specialization in particular areas of real estate.

(d) **Subject content.** On and after July 1, 1993, a provisional sales associate shall be required to successfully complete prior to the first license expiration date, forty-five (45) clock hours of post-license education or its equivalent as determined by the Commission. Such course of study shall be referred to as the Provisional Post-License Course of Real Estate, Part II of II and shall encompass the following areas of study:

(1) Real Estate Marketplace

(2) Marketing Real Estate

(3) Personal Marketing

(4) The Qualifying Process

(5) Prospecting and Negotiating

(6) Financing Real Estate, Investments and Exchanges

(7) Financial Documents

(8) Duty to Account

(9) Title Search

(10) Risk Management

(11) Broker Relationships with Parties to a Transaction

(12) Property Management

(13) Laws and Regulations Affecting Real Estate Practice

(14) Disciplinary Action

(15) Contracts.

(e) **Equivalent course content.** The Commission may approve and/or accept any offering or combination of offerings which consists of forty-five (45) clock hours or more or its equivalent as determined by the Commission provided by an entity which meets the purposes, goals and objectives of the provisional sales associate post-license education requirement.

(f) **Offerings.**

(1) The Commission may accept the following offerings as proof of meeting the post-license education requirement:

(A) Any offering which is approved and presented by those entities enumerated in Title 59, O.S., subsection B, of 858-307.2 of the "Code."

(B) Any offering in real estate, or directly related area, approved and/or accepted by the real estate regulatory agency in another state; provided such offering is not excluded elsewhere in this Chapter.

(C) Any offering in real estate, or directly related area, not accepted in paragraphs (A) or (B) of this subsection, which can be determined by the Commission to be in compliance with the intent of the rules of this Chapter.

(D) The Commission has the authority to disapprove any offering which fails to meet the purposes, goals and objectives of this Section.

(g) **Licensee responsible for notification to Commission.** Each provisional sales associate shall be responsible to furnish evidence to the Commission of having successfully completed a Commission approved forty-five (45) clock hour post-license education course or its equivalent as determined by the Commission. Upon successful completion of the post-license education requirement, evidence must be submitted on or before license expiration and on a form approved by the Commission.

(h) **Failure to complete post-license education requirement prior to license expiration.** A provisional sales associate who fails to complete the post-license education requirement prior to the first expiration date of the provisional sales associate license, shall not be entitled to renew such license.

(i) **Evidence of completion.** As evidence of having completed the education requirement, each provisional sales associate shall present one or more of the following as required by the Commission:

(1) A certificate, and/or documents, statements and forms, as may reasonably be required by the Commission, or

(2) A certified transcript; provided, however, if such offering is taken as an accredited C.E.U. (Continuing Education Unit) a certificate may be accepted in lieu of the transcript.

(j) **Attendance and successful completion required for in-class credit.** To complete any in-class offering, a person must physically be present during all of the offering time and successfully complete all course requirements and an examination.

(k) **Successful completion of materials and examination required for distance education credit.** To complete a distance education offering, a person must successfully complete all course requirements to include all modules and an examination.

(l) **Course limitations.** The following course limitations shall apply:
  (1) A provisional sales associate shall only be given credit for courses specifically approved by the Commission.
  (2) Educational courses taken for disciplinary reasons do not count towards the normal post-license education requirement.

(m) **Extension of time for completion of post-license course for provisional sales associate that has received orders for active military service.** A provisional sales associate that has received orders for active military service may request an extension of time to complete the post-license education requirement if the request is received in writing prior to the expiration of the license. The request must be accompanied by a copy of the military orders for active military service. The extension of time shall be one (1) year from the date of return from active military service. In conformance with §858-309, a licensee on active military service shall request an inactive status prior to each term for which the license is to be issued. If an extension is approved, a provisional sales associate shall be allowed to renew their license by requesting an inactive status in writing prior to each term for which the license is to be issued.

605:10-5-1. Approval of pre-license course

(a) **Course approval.** Any person or entity seeking to conduct an approved course of study shall make application and submit documents, statements and forms as may reasonably be required by the Commission. The request shall include the following:

    (1) Completed course application.

    (2) Application fee of One Hundred Twenty-five Dollars ($125.00) for each course.

    (3) An approved course syllabus encompassing the contents enumerated in 605:10-3-1 and divided by instructional periods, the name, author and publisher of the primary textbook, or a statement stating the entity will use OREC syllabus and other items as may be required by the Commission.

(b) **Course offering requirements.**

    (1) An entity not conducting an applicable approved course within any thirty-six (36) month period shall automatically be removed from approved status. In such event, the person and/or entity must re-apply as an original applicant.

    (2) If a course of study is to be conducted in the name of a corporation, the application shall include the names and addresses of all directors and officers.

    (3) An approved entity shall immediately report any changes in information in regards to the application previously filed with the Commission.

(c) **Denied applications.** No portion of the fees enumerated in this section are refundable. If an instructor, entity or course application is not approved, the applicant may appeal the decision by filing a written request for a hearing before the Commission. The hearing procedure shall be that as outlined in 605:10-1-3 titled "Appeal of administrative decisions; procedures."

(d) **Advertising course offerings.** No person or entity sponsoring or conducting a course of study shall advertise the course as approved prior to the course receiving approval from the Commission. Further, no person or entity sponsoring or conducting a course of study shall advertise that it is endorsed, recommended or accredited by the Commission although such person or entity may indicate that a course of study has been approved by the Commission.

(e) **Instructor application and approval requirements.** An individual determined by the Commission to possess one or more of the following qualifications may, upon receipt of an application and evidence of education and/or experience, be considered for approval as an approved instructor. Each application for approval must be accompanied by a Twenty-Five Dollar ($25.00) application fee and documentation required for compliance necessary to verify citizenship, qualified alien status, and eligibility under the Personal Responsibility and Work Opportunity Reconciliation Act of 1996. In order to qualify, an individual must possess proof of one of the following:

    (1) A bachelor's degree with a major in real estate from an accredited college or university.

    (2) A bachelor's degree from an accredited college or university, and at least two (2) years of applicable active experience within the previous ten (10) years as a real estate broker or sales associate.

    (3) A real estate broker or sales associate licensed in Oklahoma with a minimum of five (5) years applicable active experience within the previous ten (10) years as a real estate broker or sales associate and proof of high school education or its GED equivalent.

    (4) An individual determined by the Commission to possess a combination of education and/or applicable active broker or sales associate experience in real estate or real estate related fields which constitutes equivalent of one or more of the qualifications in paragraphs (1), (2), or (3) of this subsection.

(f) **Course content examination.** Final approval will be considered after the instructor applicant has paid the appropriate examination fee and successfully completed an applicable examination with a passing score of 80% or more. If an instructor applicant has successfully taken an applicable license examination with a passing score of 80% or more within thirty (30) days of filing an instructor application, the passing score may be utilized to meet the applicable examination requirement in this section.

(g) **Instructor renewal requirements.**

    (1) In order to maintain approved status an instructor must comply with the following:

        (A) Attend a Commission directed Instructor Renewal Course every twenty-four (24) months or successfully complete nationally recognized teacher modules consisting of at least 3 clock hours of credit as approved by the Commission.

        (B) Complete one of the following:

(i) Furnish evidence that the instructor has taught a Commission approved pre-license course, or any other real estate related course(s) the Commission determines to be equivalent, within a required thirty-six (36) month period;

(ii) Successfully pass the applicable sales or broker examination with a score of 80% or more; or

(iii) Furnish evidence to the Commission that the instructor has audited an in-class pre-license course, in its entirety, that must be validated by the school instructor or director.

(C) Any instructor not meeting the requirements of this subsection will be required to re-apply as an original instructor applicant.

(h) **Guest instructors.** Guest instructors may be utilized for in-class instruction provided an approved instructor is also present during presentations. Total guest instruction and lectures shall not consume more than thirty percent (30%) of the total course time.

(i) **Instructor and entity requirements.**

(1) **Instructor must be present.** An approved instructor must be present in the same room during all in-class course instruction for students to receive credit toward course completion.

(2) **Retention of records.** An instructor/entity shall maintain enrollment records and roll sheets which include number of hours completed by each student for seven (7) years.

(3) **Course completion certificate.** Each individual successfully completing a course of study approved by the Commission shall be furnished a certificate prescribed or approved by the Commission certifying completion. The Commission shall accept from a college or university a certified transcript or a course completion certificate as prescribed by the Commission.

(4) **Commission authorized to audit and inspect records.** A duly authorized designee of the Commission may audit any offering and/or inspect the records of the entity at any time during its presentation or during reasonable office hours or the entity may be required to provide the records to the Commission.

(5) **Clock hours and breaks.** Not more than one clock hour may be registered within any one sixty (60) minute period and no more than ten (10) minutes of each hour shall be utilized for breaks.

(6) **Class size limited.** Instructor ratio to students shall not exceed sixty (60).

(j) **Facility requirements.** The offering entity shall ensure that all classroom facilities have adequate lighting, seating space and technology to meet the needs of the student. The classroom area shall be free of distractions and noise.

(k) **Disciplinary action.** An approved course of study, director, and/or instructor may be withdrawn or disciplined as outlined in Title 59, O.S., Section 858-208, paragraph 6 either on a complaint filed by an interested person or the Commission's own motion, for the following reasons, but only after a hearing before the Commission and/or a Hearing Examiner appointed by the Commission:

(1) In the event the real estate license of a director is suspended or revoked, the course of study shall automatically be revoked.

(2) In the event the real estate license of an instructor is suspended or revoked.

(3) Failure to comply with any portion of the Code or the rules of this Chapter.

(4) Failure of an approved entity to maintain a 50% or better pass/fail ratio on the Commission examinations.

(5) Falsification of records and/or application(s) filed with the Commission.

(6) False and/or misleading advertisement.

(7) Any other improper conduct or activity of the director, instructor, or entity as may be determined by the Commission to be unacceptable.

605:10-5-1.1. Approval of a post-license course

(a) **Course approval.** In accordance with Section 858-302 of the License Code, the Commission shall determine and approve the education content of the forty-five (45) clock hour post-license course content or its equivalent. Any person or entity seeking to conduct an approved course of study shall make application and submit documents, statements and forms as may reasonably be required by the Commission. The request shall include the following:

(1) Completed course application.

(2) Application fee of One Hundred Twenty-five Dollars ($125.00) for each course.

(3) An approved course syllabus encompassing the contents enumerated in 605:10-3-7 and divided by instructional periods, with the name, author and publisher of the primary textbook.

(b) **Course offering requirements.**

(1) An offering entity not conducting the approved course within any thirty-six (36) month period shall automatically be removed from approved status. In such event, the person and/or entity must re-apply as an original applicant.

(2) If a course of study is to be conducted in the name of a corporation, the application shall include the names and addresses of all directors and officers.

(3) An approved entity shall immediately report any changes in information in regards to the application previously filed with the Commission.

(c) **Denied applications.** No portion of the fees enumerated in this Section are refundable. If an instructor, entity or course application is not approved, the applicant may appeal the decision by filing a written request for a hearing before the Commission. The hearing procedure shall be that as outlined in 605:10-1-3 titled "Appeal of administrative decisions; procedures."

(d) **Advertising course offerings.** No person or entity sponsoring or conducting a course of study shall advertise the course as approved prior to the course receiving approval from the Commission. Further, no person or entity sponsoring or conducting a course of study shall advertise that it is endorsed, recommended or accredited by the Commission although such person or entity may indicate that a course of study has been approved by the Commission.

(e) **Instructor application and approval requirements.** An individual determined by the Commission to possess one or more of the following qualifications may be considered for approval as an instructor upon receipt of an application and evidence of education and/or experience. Each application must be accompanied by a One Hundred Dollar ($100.00) application fee, and documentation required for compliance necessary to verify citizenship, qualified alien status, and eligibility under the Personal Responsibility and Work Opportunity Reconciliation Act of 1996. In order to qualify, an individual must possess proof of one of the following:

(1) Possession of a bachelor's degree in a related field.

(2) Possession of a valid teaching credential or certificate from Oklahoma or another jurisdiction authorizing the holder to instruct in an applicable field of instruction at the entity.

(3) Five (5) years full-time experience out of the previous ten (10) years in a profession, trade, or technical occupation in the applicable field of instruction.

(4) An individual determined by the Commission to possess a combination of education and/or experience in a field related to that in which the person is to instruct, which constitutes an equivalent to one or more of the qualifications in (1), (2) or (3) of subsection (e) of this section.

(f) **Instructor renewal requirements**

(1) In order to maintain approved status, an instructor must comply with the following:

(A) Attend a Commission directed Instructor Renewal Course, or its equivalent, every twenty-four (24) months. An exception to this rule may be given by the Commission if such instructor is licensed or certified through another regulatory body.

(B) Instructors approved solely for distance education courses must complete three (3) hours every twelve (12) months of instructor training as accepted by the Commission and sign a statement that changes to current law and rules have been reviewed and that the instructor has made applicable amendments to the course material.

(2) Any instructor not meeting the requirements of this subsection will be required to re-apply as an original instructor applicant.

(g) **Guest instructors.** Guest instructors may be utilized provided an approved instructor is also present during presentations. Total guest instruction and lectures shall not consume more than thirty percent (30%) of the total course time.

(h) **Instructor and entity requirements.**

(1) **Instructor must be present.** An approved instructor must be present in the same room during all course instruction for students to receive credit toward course completion.

(2) **Retention of records.** An instructor/entity shall maintain enrollment records and roll sheets which include number of hours completed by each student for a period of seven (7) years.

(3) **Course completion certificate.** Each individual successfully completing a course of study approved by the Commission shall be furnished a certificate prescribed or approved by the Commission certifying completion. The Commission shall accept from a college or university a certified transcript or a course completion certificate as prescribed by the Commission.

(4) **Course notification to Commission.** An entity conducting an approved post-license education offering shall, within seven (7) days of the completion thereof, successfully submit to the Commission the list of name(s),

license number(s) and other personal identifiers of those licensees who have successfully completed said offering. The information shall be submitted to the Commission by way of electronic format as required by the Commission, along with other information which may reasonably be required.

    (5) **Commission authorized to audit and inspect records.** A duly authorized designee of the Commission may audit any offering and/or inspect the records of the entity at any time during its presentation or during reasonable office hours or the entity may be required to provide the records to the Commission.

    (6) **Clock hours and breaks.** Not more than one clock hour may be registered within any one sixty (60) minute period and no more than ten (10) minutes of each hour shall be utilized for breaks.

    (7) **Class size limited.** Instructor ratio to students shall not exceed sixty (60).

(i) **Facility requirements.** The offering entity shall ensure that all classroom facilities have adequate lighting, seating space and technology to meet the needs of the student. The classroom area shall be free of distractions and noise.

(j) **Disciplinary action.** An approved course of study, director, and/or instructor may be withdrawn or disciplined as outlined in Title 59, O.S., Section 858-208, paragraph 6 either on a complaint filed by an interested person or the Commission's own motion, for the following reasons, but only after a hearing before the Commission and/or a Hearing Examiner appointed by the Commission:

    (1) In the event the real estate license of a director is suspended or revoked, the course of study shall automatically be revoked.

    (2) In the event the real estate license of an instructor is suspended or revoked.

    (3) Failure to comply with any portion of the Code or the rules of this Chapter.

    (4) Falsification of records and/or application(s) filed with the Commission.

    (5) False and/or misleading advertisement.

    (6) Any other improper conduct or activity of the director, instructor, or entity the Commission determines to be unacceptable.

605:10-5-2. Approval of a continuing education course

(a) **Approval and expiration of application.** An entity seeking to conduct an approved continuing education course shall make application for the approval or renewal of each course. Such approval or renewal shall expire at the end of the thirty-sixth (36) month including the month of issuance.

(b) **Application form.** Entities seeking approval of a course or group of courses totaling thirty-six (36) hours or less shall submit an application on a form prescribed by the Commission along with a nonrefundable fee of seventy dollars ($70.00). Each application is limited to thirty-six (36) hours and shall be submitted on a separate application and accompanied by a non-refundable fee of seventy dollars ($70.00). Such application shall be made on a form prescribed by the Commission. Each application shall include, but is not limited to, the following information:

    (1) The name(s), address(es), and telephone number(s) of the sponsoring entity, the owner(s), and the coordinator/director responsible for the quality of the course.

    (2) The title(s) of the course or courses.

    (3) The number of hours in each course.

    (4) A copy of each course's curriculum, including comprehensive course objectives, a detailed outline of the course subject matter and instructor(s) for each course.

    (5) The method the entity will use to evaluate the course offering.

    (6) The procedure the entity will use to monitor attendance.

    (7) A personal resume indicating name(s) and qualifications of the instructor(s).

    (8) Any other relevant information useful in determining that the entity is presenting a course which will meet the definition, purposes, goals and objectives adopted by the Commission.

    (9) A statement attesting to the fact that in accepting approval as a continuing education entity, the entity will protect and promote the purposes, goals and objectives of continuing education as stated in the License Code and Rules.

(c) **Commission course approval notice.** The Commission shall within sixty (60) days after receipt of an application inform the entity as to whether the course has been approved, denied, or whether additional information is needed to determine the acceptability of the course.

(d) **Course renewal requirements.** Upon expiration of the time period, as stated in sub-paragraph (a) of this rule, an application for renewal of any course or group of courses by an entity shall also be accompanied by a non-refundable application fee of Seventy Dollars ($70.00) for a thirty-six (36) month period. Renewal applications shall be subject to the same requirements as original applications; however, the renewal application shall be submitted prior to expiration of the course(s).

(e) **Change of information notice requirement.** Whenever there is any change in a course, the entity shall notify the Commission prior to the effective date of the change. Such change shall not be considered approved until written notice is received from the Commission.

(f) **Advertising of course offering.** An entity advertising a course as being approved for continuing education credit shall state in such advertisement, "Approved by the Commission for (correct number) hours of continuing education credit." No entity sponsoring or conducting a course of study shall advertise the course as approved prior to the course receiving approval from the Commission. Further, no entity sponsoring or conducting a course of study shall advertise that it is endorsed, recommended or accredited by the Commission.

(g) **Course requirements and limitations.**

    (1) A course will not be approved by the Commission if its duration is less than one (1) clock hour or its equivalent as determined by the Commission.

    (2) To meet the statutory requirement, a clock hour shall equal sixty (60) minutes, with no more than ten minutes of each hour utilized for breaks.

    (3) An entity conducting an approved continuing education course shall, within seven (7) days of the completion thereof, successfully submit to the Commission the list of name(s), license number(s) and other personal identifiers of those licensees who have successfully completed the course. The information shall be submitted to the Commission by way of electronic format as required by the Commission, along with other information which may reasonably be required.

    (4) Each licensee successfully completing a course shall be furnished a completion certificate, prescribed or approved by the Commission.

    (5) Each course shall be presented in a facility necessary to safely and properly present the course.

    (6) An approved instructor must be present in the same room during all in-class course instruction for students to receive credit toward course completion. If an instructor is presenting a Commission approved in-class course offering which is delivered to the licensees by way of electronic means to receiving sites other than where the instructor is presenting, the Commission may require that each receiving entity site have an in-class person monitoring the class in lieu of a Commission approved instructor.

(h) **Recruitment disallowed.**

    (1) A coordinator/director or instructor shall not allow the classroom to be used by anyone to advertise and/or recruit new affiliates for any firm. The coordinator/director shall cause the following statement to be posted in the classroom in such a manner as will be readable by all participants: "No recruiting for employment opportunities for any real estate brokerage firm is allowed in this class. Any recruiting on behalf of, or permitted by, the Instructor should be promptly reported to the Oklahoma Real Estate Commission."

    (2) An instructor shall not wear any identification relating to a specific name or identity of a real estate firm, a group of companies or franchises while in the class or on the premises.

(i) **Instructor application and approval requirements:** An individual may, upon receipt of an application and evidence of education and/or experience, be considered for approval as an instructor for a three (3) year period including the month of approval. Each application for approval must be accompanied by a Ten Dollar ($10.00) application fee. In order to qualify, an individual must possess proof of one of the following:

    (1) Possession of a bachelor's degree in a related field.

    (2) Possession of a valid teaching credential or certificate from Oklahoma or another jurisdiction authorizing the holder to instruct in an applicable field of instruction.

    (3) Five (5) years full-time experience out of the previous ten (10) years in a profession, trade, or technical occupation in the applicable field of instruction.

    (4) An individual determined by the Commission to possess a combination of education and/or experience, in a field related to that in which the person is to instruct, which constitute an equivalent to one or more of the qualifications in (1), (2) or (3) of this subsection.

(j) **Denied application; appeal.** If the Commission is of the opinion that a proposed continuing education offering does not qualify under the Code and/or Rules of the Commission, the Commission shall refuse to approve the offering and shall give notice of that fact to the party applying for approval within fifteen (15) days after its decision. Upon written request from the denied party, filed within thirty (30) days after receipt of the notice of denial, the Commission shall set the matter for hearing to be conducted within sixty (60) days after receipt of the request. The hearing procedure shall be that as outlined in 605:10-1-3, titled "Appeal of administrative decisions; procedures."

(k) **Disciplinary action.** The Commission may withdraw or discipline as outlined in Title 59, O.S., Section 858-208, paragraph 6 the approval of a coordinator/director, instructor, offering or entity either on a complaint filed by an interested person or on the Commission's own motion, for any of the following reasons, but only after a hearing before the Commission and/or a Hearing Examiner appointed by the Commission:

(1) In the event the real estate license of an instructor and/or coordinator/director is revoked or suspended.

(2) Failure to submit all documents, statements and forms as may be reasonably required by the Commission.

(3) Falsification of records and/or applications filed with the Commission.

(4) False and/or misleading advertising.

(5) Failure to revise an offering so as to reflect and present current real estate practices, knowledge, and laws.

(6) Failure to maintain proper classroom order and decorum.

(7) Any conduct which gives the coordinator/director, instructor or entity presenting the offering an unfair advantage over other brokers and/or real estate companies.

(8) Failure to comply with any portion of the Code or rules of this Chapter.

(9) Any other improper conduct or activity of the director, instructor, or entity the Commission determines to be unacceptable.

(l) **Retention of records.** An instructor/entity shall maintain enrollment records and roll sheets which include number of hours completed by each student for seven (7) years.

(m) **Commission authorized to audit.** A duly authorized designee of the Commission may audit any offering and/or inspect the records of the entity at any time during its presentation or during reasonable office hours or the entity may be required to provide the records to the Commission.

(n) **Licensee/Instructor course credit.**

(1) A licensee who is the instructor of an approved offering for continuing education shall be credited with one (1) hour for each hour of actual instruction performed.

(2) An instructor may not receive continuing education credit for instructing an offering more than one time during a license term.

(3) Records of such instruction shall be reported and maintained in the same manner as prescribed for participants elsewhere in the rules of this Chapter.

(o) **Guest instructors.** Guest instructors may be utilized for in-class instruction provided an approved instructor is also present during presentations. Total guest instruction and lectures shall not consume more than thirty percent (30%) of the total course time.

605:10-5-3. Standards for Commission approved real estate courses

(a) **Approved instructor.** Each in-class course offering shall be conducted by a Commission approved instructor. Each entity conducting a distance education course offering shall have available a Commission approved instructor. The instructor shall be available during normal business hours as posted by the instructor to answer questions about the course material and provide assistance as necessary.

(b) **Student must attend entire in-class instruction or complete all modules required for distance education instruction.** In order for an entity to certify a student as passing an approved course the student must either: (1) attend the required number of hours of in-class instruction; or (2) complete all instructional modules required for distance education instruction.

(c) **Student must successfully complete a prelicense, postlicense or distance education course offering examination.** In order for an entity to certify a student as passing an approved prelicense, postlicense or distance education course, the student must successfully complete an examination covering the contents of the course material.

(d) **Student transfers.** Except with the prior approval of the Commission, a student transferring from one course to another may not count any portion of the student's attendance or work in the former course toward passing the course. A student who enrolls in an entity which offers a Commission approved course may not transfer credit for a course or courses completed in that series to another entity unless the receiving entity offers the identical series of courses and the receiving entity agrees to accept and examine said student throughout successful completion.

(e) **Course examinations.** Each approved prelicense provisional sales associate course and postlicense course offering shall conclude with an end-of-course examination consisting of no less than two hundred (200) questions administered by the approved entity. Each approved prelicense broker course shall conclude with an end-of-course examination consisting of no less than two hundred and fifty (250) questions administered by the approved entity. Each approved distance continuing education course offering shall conclude with an end-of-course examination consisting of no less than seven (7) questions for each clock hour. End-of-course examination questions may not be the same as any previously used questions covering the respective course content.

(f) **Successful completion.** In order for a student to successfully complete a prelicense, postlicense or distance education course, the entity must require that the student complete all class material and/or modules and achieve a passing score of at least eighty percent (80%) on the entity's final examination. An entity shall require the student to complete sufficient material or modules to ensure mastery of the course offering, and shall require the student to complete the end-of-course examination. An entity may allow any student who fails to achieve a passing score the opportunity to take another examination without repeating instruction.

(g) **Grading standards.** In order for an entity to certify a student as passing an approved course, the student must meet the minimum grading standards established by this Section and the entity. On graded examinations for which this Section sets specific requirements, the entity's policy shall at least equal those requirements as listed in this Section. Other grading standards shall be in accordance with generally accepted educational standards. An entity shall publish grading standards and give them to a student in a written form at the beginning of the course.

(h) **Commission may impose sanction.** The Commission may impose any sanction permitted by law or Rules of the Commission on the approval of any entity, director and/or instructor which fails to provide proper security for their course evaluation or examination and for failing to comply with standards as set out in this Chapter.

(i) **Each entity must post notice.** Each entity must post or provide a notice that is easily observed by any person desiring to enroll in a prelicense course. The notice must at least include the following language: Oklahoma Statutes, Title 59, Section 858.301.1 "Effective November 1, 2009, state law prohibits the issuance of a real estate license to any person who has been convicted, pled guilty or pled nolo contendere to a felony for a pre-determined number of years based on the classification of said felony. For clarification, please contact the Commission and/or review the cited section of law as referenced herein. Additionally, if the applicant has delinquent unpaid child support or students loans, the applicant must check with the Real Estate Commission before enrolling in this class. The Commission will allow the applicant to seek preapproval prior to enrolling in a pre-license course."

(j) **Additional distance education course requirements.**
(1) Each course shall contain suitable learning objectives.
(2) Overview statements must be included for each course providing a quick preview of what is contained in the offering.
(3) A complete set of questions and an answer key for all examinations must be provided to the Commission with each course application. An answer key may not be included in any course materials provided to the student.
(4) From the date of enrollment, the course shall have a validity period of six (6) months in which to allow successful completion to be attained.
(5) Entities must include information with the course material that clearly informs the student of the completion time frame, passing and examination requirements, and any other relevant information necessary to complete the course.
(6) Each course must include a statement that the information presented in the course should not be used as a substitute for competent legal advice.
(7) Course offerings must be sufficient in scope and content to justify the hours requested for approval.

(k) Each entity shall promote the Basic Course of Real Estate as Part I of a two part series and the Provisional Postlicense Course of Real Estate as Part II of that series. Applicants are to be advised that Part II of the series is not to begin until after license issuance and shall be completed prior to their first license expiration.

(l) All materials that are distributed to students in any class must be current and up-to-date with the License Code and Rules and state or federal laws.

605:10-7-1. License issuance

No real estate licensee shall begin operations in the real estate business without first having been issued his or her numbered active license certificate. This includes all original licenses, activations, reinstatements and all license types being changed from a sales associate to a broker associate, or an associate to a broker or branch office broker, as defined in the rules.

605:10-7-1.1. Documentation required for compliance necessary to verify citizenship, qualified alien status, and eligibility under the Personal Responsibility and Work Opportunity Reconciliation Act of 1996

Oklahoma Real Estate Commission Rules

License renewals and reinstatements. Individuals who submit an application on or after July 1, 2002, shall be required to provide documentation necessary to verify compliance of citizenship, qualified alien status, and eligibility under the Personal Responsibility and Work Opportunity Reconciliation Act of 1996. Failure to provide this documentation shall result in disapproval of the application. If an individual fails to provide proof of citizenship within sixty (60) days from the date of reissuance of their license or approval, the individual will be placed inactive until the Commission receives current proof of citizenship or qualified alien status.

605:10-7-2. License terms and fees; renewals; reinstatements

(a) **License term and fees.** Each original license issued under the Code shall be issued to expire at the end of the thirty-sixth (36) month including the month of issuance. Each original provisional sales associate license issued under the Code shall be issued to expire at the end of the twelfth (12th) month including the month of issuance. Fees are non-refundable and are as follows:

    (1) For an original broker license and each subsequent license renewal, to include corporations, associations or partnerships, the fee shall be Two Hundred and Ten Dollars ($210.00).

    (2) For an inactive original broker license and each subsequent inactive license renewal, with the exception of corporations, associations or partnerships, the fee shall be One Hundred and Twenty-five Dollars ($125.00). In order to activate a license that was renewed inactive in the same license term, the licensee shall pay One Hundred and Thirty Dollars ($130.00). Thereafter, any future request to activate in the same license term shall be in accordance with Rule 605:10-7-4.

    (3) For an original broker associate license and each subsequent license renewal, the fee shall be One Hundred and Eighty Dollars ($180.00).

    (4) For an inactive original broker associate license and each subsequent inactive license renewal, the fee shall be One Hundred and Ten Dollars ($110.00). In order to activate a license that was renewed inactive in the same license term, the licensee shall pay One Hundred and Fifteen Dollars ($115.00) Thereafter, any future request to activate in the same license term shall be in accordance with Rule 605:10-7-4.

    (5) For an active original sales associate license and each subsequent active license renewal the fee shall be One Hundred and Fifty Dollars ($150.00).

    (6) For an inactive original sales associate license and each subsequent inactive license renewal the fee shall be Ninety-five Dollars ($95.00). In order to activate a sales associate license that was renewed inactive in the same license term, the licensee shall pay One Hundred Dollars ($100.00). Thereafter, any future request to activate in the same license term shall be in accordance with Rule 605:10-7-4.

    (7) For an original provisional sales associate license that is non-renewable the fee shall be Seventy Dollars ($70.00).

    (8) For an original branch office license and each subsequent license renewal the fee shall be One Hundred and Twenty-five Dollars ($125.00).

    (9) For each duplicate license or pocket card, where the original is lost or destroyed, and a written request is made, a fee of Seven Dollars and fifty cents ($7.50) shall be charged.

    (10) The Fifteen Dollar ($15.00) Education and Recovery Fund fee, shall be added and payable with the license fee for an original license and for each subsequent license renewal. Exceptions to this rule are: 1) a provisional sales associate license fee shall be Five Dollars ($5.00) for their twelve (12) month license term; and, 2) a branch office shall not pay the fee.

(b) **Terms cannot be altered.** Terms shall not be altered except for purposes of general reassignment of terms which might be necessitated for the purpose of maintaining an equitable staggered license term system.

(c) **Expiration date.** The actual expiration date of a license shall be midnight of the last day of the month of the designated license term. A person who allows their license to expire shall be considered an applicant and subject to a national criminal history record check, as defined by Section 150.9 of Title 74 of the Oklahoma Statutes.

(d) **Late penalty.** All renewals shall be filed on or before midnight of the tenth day of the month in which said license is due to expire, except in the event that date falls on a Saturday, Sunday or holiday; in such case, the next Commission working day shall be considered the due date for all renewals except electronic online renewal wherein this exception would not apply. Any such renewal application filed after such date shall be subject to a late penalty fee of Ten Dollars ($10.00).

(e) **Actual filing of license renewal.** A license shall lapse and terminate if a renewal application and required fees have not been filed with the Commission by midnight of the date on which the license is due to expire, except in the event that date falls on a Saturday, Sunday or holiday; in such a case, the next Commission working day shall be considered the due date. A renewal application and required fees are considered filed with the Commission on the date of the United States postal service postmark or the date personal delivery is made to the Commission office.

(f) **Reinstatement of license.** Any licensee whose license term has expired shall be considered for reinstatement of such license upon payment of an amount equal to the current examination fee in addition to the license and late penalty fee(s) for each delinquent license period(s). The following documents and fees must be submitted:

  (1) **Lapsed less than one year.** In the case of a license lapsed less than one year:
    (A) License and late penalty fee.
    (B) Reinstatement fee.
    (C) National criminal history check.
    (D) Documents as required by the Commission

  (2) **Lapsed more than one year but less than three years.** In the case of a license lapsed more than one year but less than three years:
    (A) License and late penalty fee.
    (B) Reinstatement fee.
    (C) National criminal history check.
    (D) A completed reinstatement application.
    (E) Successful completion of the appropriate licensing examination.
    (F) A statement that the applicant has read a current License Code and Rules booklet.
    (G) Documents as required by the Commission.

  (3) **Lapsed more than three years.** If an application is submitted more than three (3) years subsequent to the most recent year of licensure, the applicant shall be regarded as an original applicant.

(g) **Reinstatement of a provisional sales associate license wherein post-license education was completed prior to license expiration date.** An applicant who successfully completed the post-license education requirement before their first license expiration date and failed to renew their license on or before such date shall be eligible to reinstate the license as a sales associate according to 605:10-7-2 (f), (1) through (3).

(h) **Reinstatement of a provisional sales associate license wherein post-license education was not completed prior to license expiration date.** An applicant who has not successfully completed the post-license education requirement prior to the first license expiration date shall not be eligible to reinstate such license and shall apply and qualify as an original applicant.

(i) **Reinstatement of revoked license.** An applicant may not apply for re-license or reinstatement of license for a minimum of three (3) years from the effective date of license revocation, except for an applicant whose license was automatically revoked pursuant to Sections 858-402 or 858-604 of Title 59, Oklahoma Statutes. Upon the passage of the three (3) year period, the applicant shall be required to comply with the requirements of an original applicant.

(j) **Reinstatement of an automatically revoked license.** An applicant who has had their license automatically revoked, pursuant to Section 858-402 or 858-604 of Title 59 of the Oklahoma Statutes, shall be required to comply with the requirements of (f) of this section. In addition, reinstatement will not be granted until all outstanding amounts due the Commission have been paid in full.

(k) **Reinstatement of a surrendered or cancelled license.** A surrendered or cancelled license applicant may be reinstated provided the applicant has received approval for re-issuance from the Commission. The following forms and fees must be submitted:

  (1) **Reinstatement with term of license still current.** A surrendered or cancelled license applicant whose license term is still current:
    (A) Applicable reinstatement fee equal to the current examination fee.
    (B) Re-issuance fee equal to the transfer of license fee.
    (C) Documents as required by the Commission.
    (D) Criminal history background check.

  (2) **Reinstatement with term of license expired.** A surrendered or cancelled license applicant whose license term has expired shall be required to comply with the requirements of (f) of this section.

  (3) **Reinstatement of provisional sales associate with term of license expired.** A surrendered or cancelled provisional sales associate whose license term has expired shall be required to comply with the following:
    (A) If a provisional sales associate completed the post-license requirement on or before the first license expiration date, the applicant shall be eligible to reinstate the license according to 605:10-7-2 (f), (1) through (2).
    (B) If a provisional sales associate did not complete the post-license requirement on or before the first license expiration date, the applicant shall be required to apply and qualify as an original applicant.

(l) **Continuing education requirement.** Each licensee with the exception of those as listed in Title 59, O.S., Section 858-307.2 (D) seeking renewal of a license must submit evidence that they have completed the continuing education requirements enumerated in Section 858-307.2 of Title 59. An applicant seeking active reinstatement of a lapsed license must submit evidence that all continuing education requirements have been completed for each term in which an active license is requested.

(m) **License fees prorated.** If a real estate sales associate qualifies for a license as a real estate broker associate or broker, or if a real estate broker associate qualifies for a license as a real estate broker, the unused license fee shall be credited to the new license fee. The unused license fee credit shall commence with the first full month following the month in which the broker license is to be issued.

(n) **License expires after effective date of national criminal history check.**

(1) Any licensee who allows their license to expire shall be required to submit to a national criminal history check; however, such individual shall be allowed to proceed with reinstatement of such license pending receipt by the Commission of a completed fingerprint card, application Part A, and fee as stated elsewhere in these rules for the background search. If, the Commission does not receive a completed Part A of the application and completed finger print card and fee within thirty (30) days from the date of request by the Commission, the license will be placed inactive and a hold placed on the license until receipt by the Commission of the aforementioned items. Thereafter, upon receipt by the Commission, the license may be reactivated so long as appropriate reactivation forms and fees, as stated elsewhere in these rules, have been received by the Commission. However, if the finger print card is rejected for the purposes of a national criminal history check, the Commission will provide written notice to the licensee and the licensee must submit a new and unique fingerprint card to the Commission within thirty (30) days of receipt of such notice or the license will be placed on inactive status.

(2) A provisional sales associate who completes the Provisional Post-License Course prior to their first license expiration date but fails to timely renew the license shall be eligible to apply under the requirement under the preceding paragraph. However, after a period of three (3) years from the date of the license expiration such applicant shall no longer be eligible to apply under this section.

(o) **Issuance of license from provisional sales associate to sales associate.** A provisional sales associate is required to furnish to the Commission evidence of successful completion of the Provisional Post-license Course of Real Estate, Part II of II education requirement as set forth in Section 858-302 of Title 59, of the Oklahoma Statutes. Upon successful completion of the Provisional Post-license Course of Real Estate, Part II of II education requirement, the provisional sales associate must submit the appropriate document(s) to the Commission prior to the provisional sales associate's license expiration date for issuance of a renewable sales associate license. The Commission shall not issue the provisional sales associate a renewable sales associate license until the end of the provisional sales associate's license term and until the provisional sales associate has submitted evidence of successful completion of the forty-five (45) clock hour post-license course requirement and submitted all required form(s) and fee(s) as required by the Commission.

(p) **Active sales associate to inactive broker associate, or sales associate and/or broker associate inactive broker license - no remaining credit to be given.** In the event an active sales associate, within six (6) months of obtaining their original license, reinstatement or license renewal qualifies for an inactive broker associate license, the Commission shall not credit the difference in license fees. In the event an active sales associate or broker associate within six (6) months of obtaining their original license, reinstatement or license renewal qualifies for an inactive broker license, the Commission shall not credit the difference in the license fees.

(q) **Licensee on active duty as a member of the Armed Forces of the United States.**

(1) In accordance with Title 59, O.S., Section 4100.6 of the Post-Military Service Occupation, Education and Credentialing Act while a license holder is on active duty the license may be renewed without payment of the license and education and recovery fund fee and meeting the continuing education requirement. Such waiver shall be requested in writing to the Commission prior to license expiration along with evidence of the order for active duty. The license issued pursuant to this rule may be continued as long as the licensee is a member of the Armed Forces of the United States on active duty and for a period of at least one (1) year after discharge from active duty. Upon discharge from active duty and a request for license activation, the licensee shall submit to the Commission evidence of successful completion of the continuing education requirement for the current license renewal term.

(2) If a licensee on active duty does not request such a waiver in writing and the license expires, the applicant may, by written request provide the Commission documentation as required in subparagraph (1) of this subsection; however, no later than one (1) year after discharge from active duty.

(3) In the event a license expires during the events as noted herein, the Commission shall waive the criminal history background check and license examination.

(4) **Member of the National Guard or reserve component of the armed forces.** In accordance with Title 72, Chapter 1, Section 48.2 Extension and Renewal of Professional Licenses, any licensee whose license expires while on active duty as a member of the National Guard or reserve component of the armed forces shall be extended until no later than one (1) year after the member is discharged from active duty status. Upon the Commission receiving a copy of the official orders calling the member or reservist to active duty and official orders discharging the member or reservist from active duty all licensee fee and continuing education shall be waived for this time period as well as the criminal history background check and license examination.

(r) **Reinstatement for corporation, association or partnership.**

(1) A corporation, association or partnership that has lapsed for less than three (3) years that wishes to reinstate must submit:

(A) License and late penalty fees.

(B) Reinstatement forms and documents as required by the Commission.

(C) If the corporation or association has been lapsed for more than sixty (60) days, a current "Certification of Good Standing."

(2) Any corporation, association or partnership that has lapsed for than three (3) years must submit an original application to be considered for licensure.

(s) **Reinstatement for branch offices.**

(1) A branch office that is lapsed for less than three (3) years that wishes to reinstate must submit:

(A) License fee and late penalty fees.

(B) Reinstatement forms and documents as required by the Commission.

(2) Any branch office that has lapsed for more than three (3) years must submit an original application as a new branch office.

605:10-7-3. Placement of license on inactive status

In conformance with Section 858-309 of the Code a licensee who at any time fails to comply with all Code and Rule requirements for active license status shall be placed on inactive status. If a licensee fails to comply with a request for documentation from the Commission, based on another appropriate statutory or rule requirement which affects the license, the Commission shall place the license inactive. At any time the licensee complies with all requested requirements, the license shall be issued on active status.

605:10-7-4. Request for activation or re-issuance of license

(a) **Requirements.** All requests for activation or re-issuance of a license must be accompanied by the appropriate documents and fee of Twenty-five Dollars ($25.00) as required by the Commission. Upon activation of an inactive license wherein the licensee paid the reduced inactive license fee rate, the licensee shall be required to pay the remaining active license fee as outlined in 605:10-7-2.

(b) **Multiple change requests on same license.** In the event a licensee's request involves more than one change to the license at the same time, and each individual change requires a separate fee elsewhere in the rules of this Chapter, the Commission shall only require that one fee be charged to reissue the license if the request is done in a timely manner.

(c) **Continuing education and/or experience required for activation.** A licensee requesting activation of a license must have complied with the continuing education requirement as set forth in Section 858-307.2 of Title 59 of the Oklahoma Statutes and rule 605:10-3-6 and, if applicable, the experience requirement as set forth in Section 858-303 of Title59 of the Oklahoma Statutes and rule 605:10-3-4 and 605:10-3-4.1. Further, upon a licensee's request for activation being completed and processed, the licensee shall then be required to complete the continuing education requirement for the next license term for which the license is to be renewed active or activated.

(d) **Active status requested, however, Commission unable to activate for reasons as stated in statutes elsewhere.** In the event a licensee requests an active original license, subsequent license renewal, or activation to be issued on active status and for reasons beyond the Commission's control the licensee is unable to obtain an active license at that time, the fees as received by the Commission shall be retained and not refunded. Once the licensee corrects the problem with the appropriate regulatory agency and such agency authorizes the issuance of an active license, the Commission will then, upon receipt of an activation fee and required documentation, issue an active license.

605:10-7-5. Name changes
(a) **Name change request.** Any change of name of a licensee or licensed firm must be filed in the Commission office within ten (10) days of such change. Filed shall mean the date of the United States postal service postmark or the date personal delivery is made to the Commission office. The licensee or firm shall return the license certificate to the Commission office along with the request for such name change. Upon any request for a change of name there shall be paid a fee to the Commission of Twenty-five Dollars ($25.00) for each license to be changed. The Commission may require additional documents as may reasonably be required by the Secretary-Treasurer.
(b) **Group name changes.** Under certain circumstances as determined by the Commission, the Commission may place a cap of Seven Hundred Fifty Dollars ($750.00) on group transactions requesting licenses to be reissued. To qualify, such request must be received complete and require no further correspondence and/or documents except for the issuance of the licenses.

605:10-7-6. Certification of license history
Each request for a certification of license history shall be in the form of a letter to the Commission accompanied by a fee of Fifteen Dollars ($15.00).

605:10-7-7. Branch offices
(a) **Each additional office must be licensed.** If a broker desires to do business from more than one office location, the broker must license each additional office location as a branch office by submitting forms and fees as required by the Commission. The license shall be maintained in the branch office and available upon request.
(b) **Associate's license issued to branch office.** An associate's license shall be issued to and maintained in the office to which the associate is assigned.
(c) **Broker to designate a branch office broker to act.** A broker shall designate a branch office broker, other than himself or herself, to act as broker for each location, to supervise the activities of the branch office. The branch office shall be licensed in conformance with Section 858-310 of the Code. The branch office broker may be designated to perform all duties and sign documents on behalf of the broker with respect to the branch office at the discretion of the broker. Such designation shall be in writing and filed with the Commission. The branch office broker assumes the responsibility in conjunction with the broker, for all associates assigned to the branch office.
(d) **Broker may act as branch office broker; restriction.** A broker may act as the branch office broker if the branch office is located at the same location as the main office upon the appropriate documents and fees being filed with the Commission.
(e) **Reappointment of branch office broker.** In the event of the death, or disability of the designated branch office broker, and the branch office is to continue business, the main office broker shall appoint a new branch office broker and file the appropriate documents with the Commission within thirty (30) days of the occurrence of the event. In the event of the retirement or cessation of employment for any reason by the designated branch office broker, and the branch office is to continue business, the main office broker shall appoint a new branch office broker and file the appropriate documents with the Commission within ten (10) days of the occurrence of the event.
(f) **Branch office must utilize the same name or trade name of main office.** A branch office may utilize a trade name which is different than the main office so long as the broker registers the name(s) with the Commission.

605:10-7-8. Corporation licensing procedures and requirements of good standing
(a) **Broker license requirement.** Each corporation who performs activities which require a real estate license pursuant to Title 59, O.S., Section 858-102 of the License "Code" shall apply as a real estate broker. Upon approval by the Commission, the corporation shall be granted a real estate broker license. In order to obtain a license, the corporation shall furnish to the satisfaction of the Commission, but not limited to, the following items:
(1) Completed application form(s) and required fee(s).
(2) Verification that the corporation is authorized to transact business as a corporation in the State of Oklahoma and that the corporation is in good standing in the State of Oklahoma.
(3) Corporation must be in compliance with Title 59, O.S., Section 858-312.1 of the License "Code".
(4) Corporation must have a managing corporate broker who holds a separate license as a real estate broker.

(5) The designation of a managing corporate broker shall be established by sworn statement signed by the President of the corporation stating the date and place such action was effected.

(6) In the event of the death or disability of the managing corporate broker, the cooperation shall be required to appoint a new managing corporate broker and such notice of change must be filed in the Commission office no later than thirty (30) days of the occurrence of the event. In the event of the retirement or cessation of employment for any reason of the managing corporate broker, the corporation shall be required to appoint a new managing corporate broker and such notice of change must be filed in the Commission office no later than ten (10) working days of the occurrence of the event. The notice of change in a managing corporate broker must be accompanied by the appropriate documents as required by the Commission and a Twenty-five Dollar ($25.00) change of status fee.

(7) The corporation is to notify the Commission in writing within ten (10) days of the date of a change in corporate officers.

(b) **Corporation and managing corporate broker responsible for acts.** The managing corporate broker in conjunction with the corporation is responsible for all acts of the corporation, including the acts of all associates associated with the corporation.

(c) **Corporation closing requirements or partial ceasing of real estate activities.** When a corporation discontinues a portion of real estate activities or ceases all real estate activities, the corporation is required to comply with the following:

(1) Immediately notify the Commission.

(2) Comply with Section 605:10-13-1 (n).

(d) **Group change information.** Under certain circumstances as determined by the Commission, the Commission may place a cap of Seven Hundred Fifty Dollars ($750.00) on group transactions requesting licenses to be issued. To qualify, such request must be received complete and require no further correspondence and/or documents except for the issuance of the licenses.

605:10-7-8.1. Partnership licensing procedures and requirements of good standing

(a) **Broker license requirement.** Each partnership who performs activities which require a real estate license pursuant to Title 59, O.S., Section 858-102 of the License "Code" shall apply as a real estate broker. Upon approval by the Commission, the partnership shall be granted a real estate broker license. In order to obtain a license, the partnership shall furnish to the satisfaction of the Commission, but not limited to, the following items:

(1) Completed application form(s) and required fee(s).

(2) A written statement signed by all partners attesting to the formation of a partnership and that it is in good standing in the State of Oklahoma.

(3) Partnership must be in compliance with Title 59, O.S., Section 858-312.1 of the License "Code".

(4) Partnership must have a minimum of two managing partners who each hold a separate license as a real estate broker.

(5) The designation of the managing partners shall be established by sworn statement signed by the managing partners of the partnership stating the date and place such action was effected.

(6) In the event of the death or disability of the managing corporate broker, the cooperation shall be required to appoint a new managing corporate broker and such notice of change must be filed in the Commission office no later than thirty (30) days of the occurrence of the event. In the event of the retirement or cessation of employment for any reason of the managing partner(s), the partnership is dissolved unless the partnership agreement provides otherwise. If the partnership agreement provides for the continuation of the partnership after the loss of a partner, the partnership shall be required to appoint a new managing partner and such notice of change must be filed in the Commission office no later than ten (10) working days of the occurrence of the event. The notice of change in managing partners must be accompanied by the appropriate documents as required by the Commission and a Twenty-five Dollars ($25.00) change of status fee.

(b) **Partnership and managing partners responsible for acts.** The managing partners in conjunction with the partnership are responsible for all acts of the partnership, including the acts of all associates associated with the partnership. If a corporation or association is a partner of the partnership a letter must be submitted by the firm acknowledging that the managing member of the association or managing broker of the corporation is responsible for all acts of the partnership, including the acts of all associates associated with the partnership.

(c) **Partnership closing requirements or partial ceasing of real estate activities.** When a partnership discontinues a portion of the real estate activities or ceases all real estate activities, the partnership is required to comply with the following:
(1) Immediately notify the Commission.
(2) Comply with Section 605:10-13-1 (n).
(d) **Group change information.** Under certain circumstances as determined by the Commission, the Commission may place a cap of Seven Hundred Fifty Dollars ($750.00) on group transactions requesting licenses to be issued. To qualify, such request must be received complete and require no further correspondence and/or documents except for the issuance of the licenses.

605:10-7-8.2. Association licensing procedures and requirements of good standing

(a) **Broker license requirement.** Each association who performs activities which require a real estate license pursuant to Title 59, O.S., Section 858-102 of the License "Code" shall apply as a real estate broker. Upon approval by the Commission, the association shall be granted a real estate broker license. In order to obtain a license, the association shall furnish to the satisfaction of the Commission, but not limited to, the following items:
(1) Completed application form(s) and required fee(s).
(2) Verification that the association is authorized to transact business as an association in the State of Oklahoma and that the association is in good standing in the State of Oklahoma.
(3) Association must be in compliance with Title 59, O.S., Section 858-312.1 of the License "Code".
(4) Association must have a managing member or manager who holds a separate license as a real estate broker.
(5) The designation of a managing broker member or manager shall be established by sworn statement signed by an authorized member or manager of the association stating the date and place such action was effected.
(6) In the event of the death or disability of the managing broker member or manager, the association shall be required to appoint a new managing broker member or manager and such notice of change must be filed in the Commission office no later than thirty (30) working days of the occurrence of the event. In the event of the retirement or cessation of employment for any reason of the managing broker member or manager, the association shall be required to appoint a new managing broker member or manager and such notice of change must be filed in the Commission office no later than ten (10) working days of the occurrence of the event. The notice of change in a managing broker member or manager must be accompanied by the appropriate documents as required by the Commission and a Twenty-five Dollar ($25.00) change of status fee.
(b) **Association and managing broker member or manager responsible for acts.** The managing broker member or manager in conjunction with the association is responsible for all acts of the association, including the acts of all associates associated with the association.
(c) **Association closing requirements or partial ceasing of real estate activities.** When an association discontinues a portion of the real estate activities or ceases all real estate activities, the association is required to comply with the following:
(1) Immediately notify the Commission.
(2) Comply with Section 605:10-13-1 (n).
(d) **Limited liability company.** A limited liability company shall be considered as an association.
(e) **Group change information.** Under certain circumstances as determined by the Commission, the Commission may place a cap of Seven Hundred Fifty Dollars ($750.00) on group transactions requesting licenses to be issued. To qualify, such request must be received complete and require no further correspondence and/or documents except for the issuance of the licenses.

605:10-7-8.3. Sole Proprietor licensing procedures

(a) **Sole Proprietor.** A sole proprietor is a broker that is the sole owner of a real estate business/firm. To qualify for a sole proprietorship, the firm shall not conduct business in the name of an entity, i.e., corporation, association (Limited Liability Company) or partnership and the business/firm shall not be owned by any other person or entity. To apply as sole proprietor one must meet all requirements for a broker license and submit to the Commission the following:
(1) Completed sole proprietor broker application form(s) and fee(s) as required by the Commission.
(2) An associate release form if previously associated with a sponsoring broker.

(b) **Death, disability or retirement.** In the event of the death, disability or retirement of the sole proprietor, the sole proprietor firm shall cease business activities.

(c) **Broker responsible.** A sole proprietor broker is responsible for all acts of associates licensed with the firm.

(d) **Ceasing business activities.** When the sole proprietor discontinues a portion of the real estate activities or ceases all real estate activities, the sole proprietor is required to comply with the following:
   (1) Immediately notify the Commission.
   (2) Comply with Section 605:10-13-1 (n).

(e) **Group change information.** Under certain circumstances as determined by the Commission, the Commission may place a cap of Seven Hundred Fifty Dollars ($750.00) on group transactions requesting licenses to be issued. To qualify, such request must be received complete and require no further correspondence and/or documents except for the issuance of the licenses.

605:10-7-8.4. Managing broker, broker proprietor or branch broker's corporation or association formed for the purpose of receiving compensation

Within the meaning of subsection 14 of Section 858-312 of the "Code" payment of a commission by a broker to a managing broker's, broker proprietor's or branch broker's corporation or association does not constitute a payment of a fee (commission) to an unlicensed person provided the corporation or association and the managing broker, broker proprietor or branch broker abide by the following requirements:

   (1) The corporation or association shall not perform any act requiring a real estate license and shall not hold itself out as engaged in such activity.
   (2) The managing broker, broker proprietor or branch broker must have an active individual real estate license.
   (3) The broker of the branch broker must provide to the Commission a written statement approving of the branch broker's corporation or association.
   (4) The managing broker, broker proprietor or branch broker must be the majority stockholder and president of the corporation or majority member of the association.
   (5) Ownership of a managing broker's, broker proprietor's or branch broker's corporation or association is limited to spouses and blood relatives.
   (6) The corporation or association shall not advertise nor receive referral fees or commissions except from the broker.
   (7) The managing broker, broker proprietor or branch broker must file a written statement with the Commission including the following:
      (A) A statement that the managing broker, broker proprietor or branch broker is the majority stockholder and president of the corporation or majority member of the association.
      (B) Names and relation of all officers/members and/or stockholders.
      (C) Verification that the association or corporation is in good standing with the Oklahoma Secretary of State.

605:10-7-9. Nonresident licensing

(a) **Nonresident licensed in another jurisdiction.** A nonresident applicant may apply to the Commission for a license to operate as a nonresident by submitting all appropriate documents as required by the Commission and furnish evidence that the applicant possesses a current active license in the applicant's resident jurisdiction or another jurisdiction in which the applicant has qualified for a license. No license shall be issued to any nonresident applicant at a higher level than the highest license of any current active license in the applicant's resident jurisdiction or another jurisdiction in which the applicant has qualified for a license. All nonresidents shall be required to complete the appropriate examination as required by the Commission No inactive license experience may be credited to qualify under this section. The Commission may issue a nonresident license if such nonresident has qualified and maintains a license in another jurisdiction and meets the following qualifications:
   (1) A nonresident applicant who has been actively licensed as a sales associate or broker respectively for a minimum of two (2) years out of the previous five (5) years.
      (A) A nonresident applicant that applies under this paragraph must complete and submit the following:
         (i) Appropriate application(s).
         (ii) License certification(s) from the jurisdiction in which the applicant has held and/or currently holds a license.
         (iii) Criminal history background application, fingerprint card and fee.

        (iv) Examination fee and successful completion of the state portion of the examination.

        (v) Consent for service of jurisdiction form.

        (vi) Proof of completion of at least one (1) continuing education clock hour in each of the following Oklahoma-specific subjects: Broker Relationships Act, Contracts and Forms, and Code and Rule Updates.

    (B) Upon the Commission granting approval to the nonresident applicant for licensure in this jurisdiction, the applicant must complete and submit the following:

        (i) appropriate license application form(s) along with license and education and recovery fund fees.

  (2) A nonresident applicant who has been actively licensed less than two (2) years as a sales associate or broker respectively out of the previous five (5) years must successfully complete the appropriate examination.

    (A) A nonresident applicant applying under this paragraph must complete and submit the following:

        (i) Appropriate application(s).

        (ii) License certification(s) from jurisdiction(s) in which the applicant has held and/or currently holds a license.

        (iii) Criminal history background application, fingerprint card and fee.

        (iv) Examination fee and successful completion of the entire appropriate examination.

        (v) Consent for service of jurisdiction form.

        (vi) Proof of completion of at least one (1) continuing education clock hour in each of the following Oklahoma-specific subjects: Broker Relationships Act, Contracts and Forms, and Code and Rule Updates.

    (B) Upon the Commission granting approval to the nonresident applicant for licensure in this jurisdiction, the applicant must complete and submit the following:

        (i) Appropriate license application form(s) along with license and education and recovery fund fees.

(b) **Nonresident agreement.** The Commission may enter into a nonresident agreement with another jurisdiction and thereby qualify actively licensed nonresident applicants for licensing in this jurisdiction provided the Commission determines that the educational and experience requirements of the other jurisdiction are equivalent or equal to this jurisdiction; however, the applicant shall be required to comply with paragraph (a)(1)(A) and (B) of this section.

(c) **Nonresident applicant that is inactive in another jurisdiction.** A nonresident applicant who holds an inactive license in another jurisdiction and is unable to meet the requirement under paragraph (a) of this section may apply to the Commission for a license to operate as a nonresident provisional sales associate or broker by submitting all appropriate documents and successfully completing all requirements as required by the Commission.

  (1) The nonresident applicant must complete and submit the following:

    (A) Appropriate application(s).

    (B) Criminal history background application, fingerprint card and fee.

    (C) Qualify as an original applicant by submitting proof of appropriate required education.

    (D) Examination fee and successful completion of the entire appropriate examination.

    (E) License certification(s) from the jurisdiction(s) in which the applicant holds or has held a license.

    (F) Consent for service of jurisdiction form.

    (G) Proof of completion of at least one (1) continuing education clock hour in each of the following Oklahoma-specific subjects: Broker Relationships Act, Contracts and Forms, and Code and Rule Updates.

  (2) Upon the Commission granting approval to the nonresident applicant for licensure in this jurisdiction, the applicant must complete and submit appropriate license application form(s) along with license and education and recovery fund fees.

(d) **Consent for service of jurisdiction.** Prior to the issuance of a license to a nonresident, such nonresident shall file with the Commission a designation in writing that appoints the Secretary-Treasurer of the Commission to act as the licensed agent, upon whom all judicial and other process or legal notices directed to such nonresident licensee may be served. Service upon the agent so designated shall be equivalent to personal service upon the licensee. Copies of such appointment, certified by the Secretary-Treasurer of the Commission, shall be deemed sufficient evidence thereof and shall be admitted into evidence with the same force and effect as the original thereof. In such written designation, the licensee shall agree and stipulate that any notice or instrument which is served upon such agent shall be of the same legal force and validity as if served upon the licensee, and that the authority shall continue in force so long as any liability remains outstanding in this state. Upon receipt of any such process or notice the Secretary-Treasurer shall forthwith mail a copy of the same, by certified mail, to the last known business address of the licensee.

(e) **License history and application requirements.** Prior to the approval of the application, the nonresident must file with the Commission a certification of licensure from the real estate licensing jurisdiction of the licensee's resident jurisdiction and/or other jurisdictions in which the applicant has held or currently holds a license. The applicant shall pay the Commission the same examination fee and license fee as provided in the "Rules" for the obtaining of a resident sales associate or broker license in this jurisdiction. The certification of licensure shall be valid for sixty (60) days from date of issuance.

(f) **Approved application valid for ninety (90) days.** An approved application shall be valid for ninety (90) days.

(g) **Stipulations.** Nonresident licenses granted under the provisions of this section shall remain in force, only as long as such nonresident remains licensed in good standing in this jurisdiction or any other jurisdiction in which the nonresident is or has been licensed.

(h) **Co-brokerage arrangements.** A broker of this jurisdiction may participate in a cooperative brokerage arrangement with a broker of another jurisdiction provided that each broker conducts real estate activities only in the jurisdiction in which they are licensed.

(i) **Request for license transfer.** In the event a nonresident Oklahoma licensee desires to transfer the license and obtain a resident Oklahoma license or desires to transfer the license to another jurisdiction, the nonresident licensee shall be required to meet all applicable requirements and pay the appropriate change of address fee and submit all appropriate documents as required by the Commission. In the event a resident Oklahoma licensee desires to transfer the license and obtain a nonresident Oklahoma license, the licensee shall be required to pay the appropriate change of address fee and complete and submit all appropriate documents as required by the Commission.

(j) **Continuing education.** If a nonresident licensee completes the continuing education requirement of another jurisdiction for license renewal, the Commission will require proof of completion of at least one (1) continuing education clock hour in each of the following Oklahoma-specific subjects for license renewal: Broker Relationships Act, Contracts and Forms, and Code and Rule Updates. If a nonresident licensee is exempt from meeting a continuing education requirement in another jurisdiction then the licensee must meet the Oklahoma continuing education requirement as follow:

(1) Each licensee shall have completed of said twenty-one (21) clock hours of continuing education six (6) clock hours of required subject matter as directed by the Commission

(2) The required subject matter, or its equivalent, as determined by the Commission, shall consist of all following subjects each license term: Professional Conduct, Broker Relationships Act, Fair Housing, Contracts and Forms, Code and Rules Updates and Current Issues. The remaining fifteen (15) clock hours may consist of elective subject matter as approved by the Commission

(3) Any licensee may complete the Broker in Charge course as approved by the Commission consisting of fifteen (15) clock hours in lieu of the required subject matter.

(4) Any Broker who holds or has held a license type of Broker Manager (BM), Proprietor Broker (BP), or Branch Broker (BB) during any portion of their current license term shall be required to successfully complete the Broker in Charge course as approved by the Commission consisting of fifteen (15) clock hours, or its equivalent, as approved by the Commission. In addition, to complete the continuing education requirement of twenty-one (21) clock hours such broker shall complete at least two (2) of the six (6) required subject matter, equal to at least six (6) clock hours, as referenced in paragraph (2) of this subsection.

(5) Any broker that lapsed or renewed inactive in their previous license term or current license term who applies for reinstatement or activation and held in their previous or current license term the license type of Broker Manager (BM), Proprietor Broker (BP), or Branch Broker (BB) must complete the Broker in Charge course and two (2) of the six (6) required subject matter totaling six (6) hours prior to their license being reinstated active or reactivating.

605:10-7-10. Resident applicants currently or previously licensed in other jurisdictions

(a) **Requirements.** In order to qualify under previously licensed procedures, an applicant must complete and submit all appropriate documents as required by the Commission and furnish evidence that the applicant possesses or has possessed a license in good standing in another jurisdiction. Applications approved for resident applicants currently or previously licensed in other jurisdictions shall be valid for ninety (90) days. The Commission may issue the applicant a license if such previously licensed applicant meets all of the requirements of either paragraphs (1), (2), (3) or (4) of this subsection:

(1) If a nonresident agreement exists between Oklahoma and the jurisdiction in which the applicant qualified for a license, the Commission shall qualify the licensed applicant through the nonresident agreement. In order to

qualify under this paragraph an individual must furnish evidence that the license from the former jurisdiction has not been inactive more than six (6) months prior to application to this jurisdiction.

(A) An applicant applying under this paragraph must complete and submit the following:
  (i) Appropriate application(s).
  (ii) License certification(s) from the jurisdiction(s) in which the applicant has held or currently holds a license.
  (iii) Criminal history background application, fingerprint card and fee.
  (iv) Examination fee and successful completion of the state portion of the examination.
  (v) Proof of completion of at least one (1) continuing education clock hour in each of the following Oklahoma-specific subjects: Broker Relationships Act, Contracts and Forms, and Code and Rule Updates.

(B) Upon the Commission granting approval to the applicant for licensure in this jurisdiction, the applicant must complete and submit the appropriate license application form(s) along with license and education and recovery fund fees.

(C) An applicant qualifying under this paragraph will be issued either a sales associate, broker associate or broker license.

(2) If a nonresident agreement does not exist, the applicant shall be required to furnish evidence of two (2) years of active experience respectively as a sales associate or broker out of the previous five (5) years. In order to qualify under this paragraph an individual must furnish evidence that the license from the former jurisdiction has not been inactive more than six (6) months prior to application to this jurisdiction.

(A) An applicant applying under this paragraph must complete and submit the following:
  (i) Appropriate application(s).
  (ii) License certification(s) from the jurisdiction(s) in which the applicant has held or currently holds a license.
  (iii) Criminal history background application, fingerprint card and fee.
  (iv) Examination fee and successful completion of the state portion of the examination.
  (v) Proof of completion of at least one (1) continuing education clock hour in each of the following Oklahoma-specific subjects: Broker Relationships Act, Contracts and Forms, and Code and Rule Updates.

(B) Upon the Commission granting approval to the applicant for licensure in this jurisdiction, the applicant must complete and submit the appropriate license application form(s) along with license and education and recovery fund fees.

(C) An applicant qualifying under this paragraph will be issued either a sales associate, broker associate or broker license.

(3) An applicant who does not possess the required two (2) years active experience out of the previous five (5) years respectively as a sales associate or broker, or an applicant who does not meet all of the requirements of either paragraphs (1) or (2) of this subsection, shall be required to apply as an original applicant.

(A) An applicant applying under this paragraph must complete and submit the following:
  (i) Qualify as an original applicant by submitting appropriate required education and application.
  (ii) License certification(s) from the jurisdiction(s) in which the applicant has held or currently holds a license.
  (iii) Criminal history background application, fingerprint card and fee.
  (iv) Examination fee and successful completion of the entire appropriate examination.
  (v) Proof of completion of at least one (1) continuing education clock hour in each of the following Oklahoma-specific subjects: Broker Relationships Act, Contracts and Forms, and Code and Rule Updates.

(B) Upon the Commission granting approval to the applicant for licensure in this jurisdiction, the applicant must complete and submit the appropriate license application form(s) along with license and education and recovery fund fees.

(C) An applicant qualifying under this paragraph will be issued either a provisional sales associate, broker associate or broker license.

(4) In accordance with Title 59, O.S., Section 4100.4 of the Post-Military Service Occupation, Education and Credentialing Act, the Commission shall, upon satisfactory evidence of equivalent education, training and experience by an applicant for licensure, accept the education, training and experience completed by the applicant as a member of the Armed Forces or Reserves of the United States, National Guard of any

jurisdiction, the Military Reserves of any jurisdiction, or the Naval Militias of any jurisdiction, and apply it in the manner most favorable toward satisfying the applicant's qualifications for examination and license issuance.

    (A) An applicant applying under this paragraph must complete and submit the following:

        (i) Appropriate application(s).

        (ii) Satisfactory evidence of education, training and experience obtained by the applicant as a member of the military Armed Forces or Reserves of the United States.

        (iii) License certification(s) from the jurisdiction(s) in which the applicant has held or currently holds a license.

        (iv) Criminal history background application, fingerprint card and fee.

        (v) Examination fee and successful completion of the entire appropriate examination.

    (B) Upon the Commission granting approval to the applicant for licensure in this jurisdiction, the applicant must complete and submit the appropriate license application form(s) along with license and education and recovery fund fees.

    (C) An applicant qualifying under this paragraph will be issued either a provisional sales associate, broker associate or broker license.

(b) **May be required to meet additional requirements.** If, in the opinion of the Commission, there is question as to the competence of the previously licensed applicant, the individual may be required to meet additional educational courses and/or successfully complete the Oklahoma examination.

(c) Military spouse applicant - 120 day temporary permit. In accordance with Title 59, O.S., Section 4100.5 the Commission shall expedite the issuance of a 120 day permit to an applicant:

    (1) Who is actively licensed in real estate in another jurisdiction;

    (2) Whose spouse is an active-duty member of the Armed Forces or Reserves of the United States;

    (3) Whose spouse is subject to military transfer to this state; and

    (4) Who left employment in another state to accompany their spouse to this state.

Expedite licensure means to issue the applicant a temporary permit to perform licensed activities for a period of 120 days to allow the person to successfully complete all application requirements as required by the Commission and any specific requirements in this state that were not required in the jurisdiction in which the person was licensed, i.e., criminal history background check and successful passage of the Oklahoma portion of the examination. An extension of the 120 days may be granted up to an additional 60 days if written justification is submitted by the applicant to the commission and the delay of license issuance was not the fault of the applicant.

605:10-9-1. Place of business and broker requirements

(a) **Place of Business.** Each broker shall maintain a specific place of business, and supervise a brokerage practice which is available to the public during reasonable business hours. Each broker shall be available to manage and supervise such brokerage practice and comply with the following:

    (1) The broker's license, as well as those of all licensees associated with the broker, must be maintained in the place of business as registered with the Commission and available upon request.

    (2) The place of business shall consist of at least one enclosed room or building of stationary construction wherein negotiations and closing of real estate transactions of others may be conducted and carried on with privacy and wherein the broker's books, records and files pertaining to real estate transactions of others are maintained.

    (3) Each broker shall register for each place of business a physical address and office telephone number.

(b) **Branch offices.** If a broker maintains one or more places of business, the additional places of business shall be referred to as a branch office. Each associate's license shall be issued to and available upon request in the office to which the associate is assigned whether that be the main place of business or branch office.

(c) **Office located at residence.** The office may be in the residence of the broker.

(d) **Associates not permitted to have an office.** Associates are not permitted to have a place of business, but must be registered with a place of business maintained and registered in the name of the broker.

(e) **Licenses issued to place of business.** All licenses will be issued to the street address of the place of business, unless the United States postal service refuses to deliver mail when addressed in such manner.

(f) **Broker may be broker for more than one firm.** A broker may be the broker for more than one firm so long as the firms are at the same location.

(g) **Broker is responsible for acts of unlicensed assistants.** A broker is responsible for all real estate related activities of any unlicensed assistant working within the firm.

605:10-9-2. Office identification

(a) **Office identification sign.** Each licensed real estate broker holding an active license certificate, except those registered as being associated with a broker who is in compliance with this Section, shall erect and maintain a sign on or about the entrance of his or her office and all branch offices, which sign shall be easily observed and read by persons about to enter any of said offices.

(b) **Specifications of sign.** Each sign shall contain the name of the broker or trade name registered with the Commission, and if a partnership, association or corporation, shall contain the name or trade name of such firm. The sign must indicate that the party is a real estate broker and not a private party, to include, but not limited to, "company", "realty", or "real estate", as the case may be, all in letters not less than one (1) inch in height. Legal abbreviations following the trade name or name under which the broker is licensed shall be acceptable as long as they are easily identifiable by the public as such.

605:10-9-3. Trade names

Each licensed broker or entity must register in writing to the Commission all trade names used in connection with real estate activities prior to the trade name being advertised or displayed in any way. Further, each broker is to notify the Commission in writing of all deleted or unused trade names.

605:10-9-3.2. Team registration and fees.
  (a) The broker shall register each team within the brokerage with the Commission on a form prescribed by the Commission. The fee for each team name registration shall be $100.00.
  (b) Each team name must be approved by the broker and must be unique and not registered to another real estate team within the State of Oklahoma, and must not be identical to any association, corporation or partnership licensed as a real estate entity by the Commission.
  (c) The broker shall not allow any team name identical to an associate's corporation or association formed for the purpose of receiving compensation.
  (d) Each team name must be registered to the Commission prior to the performance of any licensable activities by the team.
  (e) It shall be prohibited for a broker to register any team name that is not being used by a team within their brokerage.
  (f) The broker shall maintain and keep current a list of teams and their respective members, in writing, within the brokerage. Copies of this list shall be made available immediately to the Commission upon request.
  (g) The broker shall notify the Commission, in writing, of all deleted or unused team names.

605:10-9-4. Advertising
(a) **Requirements and prohibitions.**
  (1) A broker, when advertising, must use their registered business trade name or the name under which the broker is licensed; however, yard signs must also include the broker's office telephone number. A firm shall not register or use a trade name of another licensed firm. In addition, the advertisement must indicate that the party is a real estate broker and not a private party, to include, but not limited to, "agency", "company", "realty", or "real estate", as the case may be. Legal abbreviations following the trade name or name under which the broker is licensed shall be acceptable as long as they are easily identifiable by the public as such.
  (2) No real estate advertisement shall show only a post office box number, telephone number or street address.
  (3) A broker, when operating under a franchise name, shall clearly reveal in all office identification and in all advertising other than institutional type advertising designed to promote a common name, the franchise name along with the name of the broker or business trade name as registered with the Commission. A franchise name shall not be the complete business trade name. All institutional type franchise advertising shall indicate that each office is independently owned and operated.
  (4) A licensee shall not advertise, either personally or through any media, to sell, buy, exchange, rent, or lease property when such advertisement is directed at or referred to persons of a particular race, color, creed, religion, national origin, familial status or handicap. The contents of any advertisement must be confined to information relative to the property itself, and any advertisement which is directed at or referred to persons of any particular race, color, creed, religion, national origin, familial status, age or handicap is prohibited.
  (5) Any advertising in any media which is misleading or inaccurate in any material fact or in any way misrepresents any property, terms, values, services, or policies is prohibited.
  (6) A licensee shall not advertise any property for sale, rent, lease, or exchange in any media unless the broker has first secured the permission of the owner or the owner's authorized representative and said permission has a definite date of expiration.
  (7) **Social networking.** A licensee who is engaged in licensed activities through social networking mediums must indicate their license status and include their broker's reference as required elsewhere in this rule.
  (8) A licensee shall not use a yard sign at the licensee's personal residence as a marketing tool, to make it appear the real property is for sale, lease or rent when such is not the case.
  (9) A broker may, or authorize an associate to, promote a seller incentive with the consent of the seller. The publicity must clearly indicate the incentive is being offered by the seller and not by the licensee and that the promotion only applies to a seller's particular property or properties.
(b) **Associates advertising.**
  (1) An associate is prohibited from advertising under only the associate's name.
  (2) All advertising by an associate must be under the direct supervision of the associate's broker.
  (3) In all advertising, the associate must include the name of the associate's broker or the name under which the broker operates, in such a way that the broker's reference is prominent, conspicuous and easily identifiable. If approved by a broker, an associate may include in the advertisement:

      (A) The associate's personal insignia of which such approval is to be maintained by the broker and which cannot be construed as that of a firm's name.

      (B) The associate's personal nickname or alias which must be registered at the Commission prior to its use and which cannot be construed as that of a firm's name.

      (C) An associate's contact information.

      (D) A slogan which cannot be construed as that of a firm's name.

      (E) A domain/website name that is registered with the broker. Within this domain/website, the broker's reference shall appear on every individual page and/or frame.

   (4) An associate's contact information may be added to a yard sign if the yard sign contains the registered name or trade name and office telephone number of the broker so long as it is approved by the broker.

   (5) Open house or directional signs used in conjunction with broker's signs do not have to contain the name or trade name of the associate's broker and broker's telephone number.

(c) Team advertising.

   (1) A team is prohibited from advertising only under the team name.

   (2) All advertising by a team must be under the direct supervision of the team's broker.

   (3) All team advertising must include the name of the team's broker or the name under which the broker operates, in such a way that the broker's reference is prominent, conspicuous and easily identifiable. If approved by the broker, a team may include in the advertisement:

      (A) The team's personal insignia of which such approval is to be maintained by the broker.

      (B) The team's contact information.

      (C) A team slogan approved by the broker.

      (D) A domain/website name that is registered with the broker. Within this domain/website, the broker's reference shall appear one very individual page and/or frame.

(d) Licensee acting as owner, purchaser or direct employee of owner.

   (1) When a licensee, either active or inactive, is purchasing real estate or is the owner of property that is being sold, exchanged, rented or leased and such is being handled either by the licensee or marketed through a real estate firm, the licensee is required to disclose in writing on all documents that pertain to the transaction and in all advertisements that he or she is licensed. On all purchase or lease contracts the licensee is to include their license number.

   (2) A licensee who is not acting in the capacity of a licensee but is engaged in buying, selling, leasing or renting real estate as a direct employee for the owner or as an officer for an entity is not required to indicate in the advertising that he or she is licensed.

605:10-9-5. Broker change of address or office telephone number

(a) **Change of business address or office telephone number.** Any change of business address or office telephone number of a broker must be filed in the Commission office within ten (10) days of such change. Filed shall mean the date of the United States Postal Service postmark or the date personal delivery is made to the Commission office. The broker shall return his or her certificate to the Commission along with those of all licensees in his or her association with a request for a change of address. Upon any request for a change of address there shall be paid a fee to the Commission of Twenty-five Dollars ($25.00) for each license to be changed. No fee shall be charged for adding or deleting an office telephone number.

(b) **Group change of address.** Under certain circumstances as determined by the Commission, the Commission may place a cap of Seven Hundred Fifty Dollars ($750.00) on group transactions requesting licenses to be issued. To qualify, such request must be received complete and require no further correspondence and/or documents except for the issuance of the licenses.

(c) **Change of home address.** A broker is required to notify the Commission of his or her current home address. Such change shall be filed in the Commission office within ten (10) days of such change. No fee is required to change the licensee's record; however, a fee of Twenty-five Dollars ($25.00) will be charged if the change requires a new license to be issued.

605:10-9-6. Death or disability of broker

    Upon the death or inability of a broker to act as a broker the following procedures shall apply:

(1) In the case of a corporation, association or partnership, the provisions of 605:10-7-8 relating to corporations, 605:10-7-8.2 relating to associations, and 605:10-7-8.1 relating to partnerships shall apply.

(2) In the case of a sole proprietor all brokerage activity must cease and a family attorney or representative should perform the following:

    (A) Notify the Commission in writing of the date of death or disability.

    (B) Advise the Commission as to the location where records will be stored. Such records may be assigned to another broker.

    (C) Return the broker's license certificate and pocket identification card and all license certificates of those associated with the broker to the Commission and advise the Commission as to the circumstances involving any not returned.

    (D) Notify each listing and management client in writing that the broker is no longer in business and that the client may enter a new listing or management agreement with the firm of his or her choice.

    (E) Notify each party and co-broker to any existing contracts.

    (F) Retain trust account monies under the control of the administrator, executor or co-signer on the account until such time as all parties to each transaction agree in writing to disposition or until a court of competent jurisdiction issues an order relative to disposition.

    (G) Notify the Commission of the date the trust account will be closed.

    (H) All advertising in the name of the firm must be terminated and offering signs removed within thirty (30) days of death or disability of the broker.

(3) In the case of a corporation, association or partnership which ceases all brokerage activity, the provisions of paragraph (2) of this Section apply.

605:10-9-7. Requirements for cessation of real estate activities

(a) **Requirement.** Unless specifically approved otherwise by the Commission a real estate firm shall, when ceasing a portion of real estate activities or ceasing all real estate activities, comply with Section 605:10-13-1 (m).

(b) **Ceasing a portion of real estate activities.** To cease a portion of real estate activities refers to closing a department within a firm wherein, to include but not limited to, separate accounting, trust/escrow accounts and trade names were established and utilized.

(c) **Firm not active in performing real estate activities.** If a firm is not active in performing real estate activities, such firm shall comply with Section 605:10-13-1 (m), (1), (A) through (C.)

605:10-9-8. Branch office closing instructions

The Commission must receive in writing, the requirements listed in this Section at the time notice is given to the Commission that the branch office has closed; however, a written request may be submitted to the Commission for approval to extend the period for submitting such documents and information. Unless specifically approved otherwise by the Commission, a real estate branch office shall be closed by the main office broker in the following manner:

(1) Notify the Commission in writing of the date the branch office will close and advise as to the location where records will be stored and retained for a minimum of five (5) years in conformance with 605:10-13-1 (1).

(2) Return the branch office license certificate and pocket identification card along with all license certificates of those associated with the branch office to the Commission and advise the Commission as to the circumstances involving any not returned.

(3) Release forms must be filed for all licensees affiliated with the branch office.

(4) The branch office broker must either transfer his or her license to a firm of his or her choice or place his or her license on inactive status.

(5) If the main office is not going to service the branch office's existing listing and management clients, as well as parties and co-brokers to existing contracts, notice is to be sent in writing advising all parties of the date the branch office will close and advise each client that he or she may enter a new listing or management agreement with a firm of his or her choice.

(6) All advertising in the name of the branch office must be terminated and offering signs removed within thirty (30) days of office closing.

(7) Trust account funds and pending contracts must be maintained by the responsible broker until final proper disbursal or until new agreements are secured from all parties for transfer of the funds and/or contracts. The Commission is to be notified in writing of any accounts that are closed.

605:10-11-1. Acts of associates

(a) **Requirement.** All acts performed by an associate under the provisions of the "Real Estate License Code" shall be done only in the name of the associate's broker.

(b) **Limitation.** An associate shall not be allowed to work for more than one broker at the same time.
    (1) An exception to this subsection would be if the associate's broker agreed to loan the associate to another broker for a specific duty to be performed, such as:
        (A) Sitting at an open house.
        (B) Calling an auction or performing other auction related duties.
        (C) Any other specific duty as requested in writing and approved by the Commission.
    (2) The broker is responsible for all acts performed by the associate while the associate is performing a specific duty for another broker.

(c) **An associate is responsible for acts of unlicensed assistants.** An associate who employs an unlicensed assistant is responsible in conjunction with the broker for all real estate related activities of the unlicensed assistant.

605:10-11-2. Associate licenses

(a) **License issuance and change request.** Each associate license shall be issued to the associate's broker, who shall retain custody of such license. Upon an associate leaving the association of the broker, the associate's license shall be returned to the Commission, together with a release executed by the broker. Any change of association from one firm to another or relocation from one office to another within a firm by an associate must be filed in the Commission office within ten (10) days. The associate's new broker shall be required to file a consent agreement to sponsor said associate on a form provided by the Commission. An associate requesting an association or office change shall be required to pay a fee of Twenty-five Dollars ($25.00).

(b) **Broker refusal to release associate.** In the event a broker refuses for any reason to release an associate, the associate shall notify the broker by certified mail of the disassociation and furnish the Commission a sworn statement that the notification has been sent to the broker. Upon receipt by the Commission of the aforementioned statement, the Commission shall release the licensee.

(c) **Group change requests.** Under certain circumstances as determined by the Commission, the Commission may place a cap of Seven Hundred Fifty Dollars ($750.00) on group transactions requesting licenses to be reissued. To qualify, the request must be received complete and require no further correspondence and/or documents except for the issuance of the licenses.

(d) **Associates transfer.** When an affiliated associate leaves a broker for whom the associate is acting, the broker shall immediately cause the license of that associate to be forwarded to the Commission along with a release of association form. The broker shall make every attempt to notify the associate of the disassociation.

(e) **Active associate may continually act.** An active associate transferring from one broker to a new broker may continually act if the change is done in a timely manner and in compliance with the ten (10) day notification requirement and other applicable rules of this Chapter.

(f) **Compensation due a disassociated associate.** A previous broker may pay compensation due a disassociated associate directly to the associate and not be required to make such payment through the associate's new broker. However, any agreements between the associate and prior broker requiring further activities to be performed in connection with the compensation to be received, can only be performed with consent and acknowledgement of the new broker.

(g) **Change of home address.** An associate is required to notify the Commission office of his or her current home address. The change shall be filed in the Commission office within ten (10) days of the change. No fee is required to change the licensee's records; however a fee of Twenty-five Dollars ($25.00) will be charged if the change requires a new license to be issued.

605:10-11-3. Associate's corporation or association formed for the purpose of receiving compensation

Within the meaning of subsection 14 of Section 858-312 of the "Code" payment of a commission by a broker to an associate's corporation or association does not constitute a payment of a fee (commission) to an unlicensed person provided the corporation or association, the associate and the broker, abide by the following requirements:
    (1) The associate's corporation or association shall not perform any act requiring a real estate license and shall not hold itself out as engaged in such activity.

(2) The associate must have an active individual real estate license.

(3) The broker of the associate must provide the Commission a written statement approving of the associate's corporation or association.

(4) The associate must be the majority stockholder and president of the corporation or majority member of the association.

(5) Ownership of an associate's corporation or association is limited to spouses and blood relatives.

(6) The associate's corporation or association shall not advertise nor receive referral fees or commissions except from the associate's broker.

(7) The broker and associate must complete and sign a Commission approved form that includes the following:

    (A) A statement that the associate is the majority stockholder and president of the corporation or majority member of the association.

    (B) Names and relation of all officers/members and/or stockholders.

    (C) Verification that the association or corporation is in good standing with the Oklahoma Secretary of State.

605:10-13-1. Duty to account; broker

(a) **Deposit and account of trust/escrow funds.**

(1) The obligation of a broker to remit monies, valuable documents and other property coming into his or her possession within the meaning of subparagraph six (6), Section 858-312 of the "Code" shall be construed to include, but shall not be limited to, the following:

    (A) Shall deposit all checks and monies of whatever kind and nature belonging to others in a separate account in a financial institution wherein the deposits are insured by an agency of the federal government.

    (B) The broker is required to be a signor on the account.

    (C) The account must be in the name of the broker as it appears on the license or trade name as registered with the Commission and styled as a trust or escrow account and shall be maintained by the broker as a depository for deposits belonging to others.

    (D) All escrow funds shall be deposited before the end of the third banking day following acceptance of an offer by an offeree unless otherwise agreed to in writing by all interested parties.

    (E) The broker shall maintain such funds in said account until the transaction involved is consummated or terminated and proper accounting made.

    (F) The broker shall at all times, maintain an accurate and detailed record thereof.

(2) Funds referred to in this subsection shall include, but are not limited to earnest money deposits, money received upon final settlements, rents, security deposits, money advanced by buyer or seller for the payment of expenses in connection with closing of real estate transactions, and money advanced by his or her principal or others for expenditures on behalf of subject principal.

(b) **Commingling prohibited.** A broker may not keep any personal funds in the trust account except amounts sufficient to insure the integrity of the account and cover any charges made by the financial institution for servicing the trust or escrow account.

(c) **Interest bearing account.** A broker shall not be prohibited from placing escrow monies in an interest bearing account; however, he or she must disclose in writing to all parties that the account bears interest and identify the party receiving the interest. The Commission does not prohibit the broker from receiving the earned interest. In the event the interest is credited to the broker, the broker should, upon final consummation of the transaction, immediately disburse the interest from the account or insure that the amount does not exceed a reasonable amount to cover normal financial institution charges. The broker is required to maintain complete and accurate records of the interest earned. The interest bearing account must be a demand type account; this prohibits the use of certificate of deposit or other types of time deposits as trust/escrow accounts.

(d) **Trust account not mandatory unless funds or items are held.** A broker shall not be required to maintain a trust or escrow account unless monies or other depositable items belonging to others are accepted by the broker and require the broker to place the monies or items in the broker's trust account.

(e) **Trust accounts must be registered with commission.** A broker shall be required to notify the Commission in writing of all trust or escrow accounts, security deposit accounts, rental management operating accounts, and interest bearing accounts in which trust funds are held. Further, if a broker is a signor on a principal's account, the broker shall register that account as a trust account. A broker shall inform the Commission in writing of any accounts which are closed and no longer in use.

(f) **Settlement statement to be furnished.** A broker shall insure that a signed settlement statement is furnished in each real estate transaction wherein he or she acts as broker, at the time such transaction is consummated.

(g) **Payment of funds.** A broker shall pay over all sums of money held by him or her promptly after the closing of any transaction, provided, that upon any hearing to suspend or revoke his or her license under this Section, the failure to pay over any sums of money held by him or her within three (3) days after a closing shall be prima facie evidence of a violation by such person under the provisions of this Section.

(h) **Return of earnest money or items.** In the event a transaction does not consummate, a broker shall promptly disburse the earnest money or items to the proper party in accordance with the terms of the contract. In the event a dispute arises prior to the disbursement, the broker shall follow rule 605:10-13-3 or may file an interpleader action with the appropriate court.

(i) **Documents, items, or monies furnished to all parties.** A broker shall insure the timely delivery or return of all documents, items or monies to a party to a transaction wherein the broker or the broker's associate have provided services.

(j) **Inform all parties pertaining to escrow being held.** A broker shall insure that all parties of each transaction are informed of the details relating to the escrow including, but not limited to, a statement as to the nature of a non-depositable item, the value of the item, and in whose custody the item is being placed.

(k) **Bookkeeping system required.** A broker shall maintain a bookkeeping system i.e., canceled checks, check book, deposit receipts, general accounts ledger, etc. which will accurately and clearly disclose full compliance with the Law relating to the maintaining of trust accounts.

(l) **Record retention.** A broker shall maintain all records and files for a minimum of five (5) years after consummation or termination of a transaction. In the case of trust account records the five years shall commence with the date of disbursal of funds. Records as referenced in this paragraph shall be destroyed in a secure manner.

(m) **Requirements for storage of records on alternative media.** The Real Estate Commission establishes the following requirements for storage of trust account and transaction records stored on alternative media. Alternative media is defined as media that uses an electronic device to store or retrieve the information that pertains to the trust account and transaction documentation. This requirement applies to any computer technology utilized by the broker to create, store or retrieve the aforementioned documentation, whether the computerized device is internal or external to the broker's computer equipment. If a broker utilizes his own equipment or a third party vendor to create, store or retrieve this information, the broker shall ensure that the documentation is maintained and able to be retrieved for the five (5) year time period as required by the Commission.

 (1) Trust account records shall be maintained by the broker in their original format for a minimum of two (2) years. Trust account records may then be transferred to an alternative media for the remaining required record retention time.

 (2) Records, with the exception of trust account records, may be transferred at any time to an alternative media for the remaining required retention time.

 (3) After documents are converted to alternative media, a quality assurance check shall be done to ensure that every document was imaged and can be reproduced in a legible and readable condition on a display device.

 (4) After the quality assurance check is completed, the original documents may be destroyed.

 (5) A broker shall maintain the alternative media and a means of viewing and retrieving records, and shall provide a true, correct and legible paper copy to the Commission upon request.

 (6) A broker shall store copies of the alternative media and the equipment used to read the media in an environment and at a level of quality conducive to maintain the ability to reproduce the media throughout the retention period. Reproduce means a process in which a document can be converted from the alternative media to a paper copy that is legible and able to be read.

(n) **Cessation of real estate activities.** Upon a firm ceasing a portion of real estate activities or ceasing all real estate activities the broker shall:

 (1) Notify the Commission in writing of the effective date of such action and advise as to the location where records will be stored and comply with the following:

  (A) Return the broker's license certificate and pocket identification card and all license certificates of those associated with the broker to the Commission and advise the Commission as to the circumstances involving any not returned.

  (B) Release forms must be filed for all licensees affiliated with the firm.

  (C) The broker must either transfer to a new firm or place his or her license on inactive status.

 (2) Notify in writing all listing and management clients, as well as parties and co-brokers to existing contracts advising them of the date of cessation of real estate activities.

(3) All advertising in the name of the firm must be terminated and offering signs removed within thirty (30) days of cessation of real estate activities.

(4) Funds in trust accounts and pending contracts must be maintained by the responsible broker until consummation of transaction and final proper disbursal of funds. Upon final disbursements of funds the broker is required to close the account and notify the Commission in writing that the account is closed.

(5) In the event the responsible broker is unable to continue to maintain the funds and/or pending contracts, funds and/or pending contracts may be transferred to another authorized broker, entity or legal representative until consummation and proper disbursal of funds. In this event, the broker must submit a request in writing to the Commission for approval to transfer the contracts and/or funds. Upon written approval by the Commission, the broker must secure approval and obtain new agreements from all parties for transfer of the contracts and/or funds.

(6) If funds, items and/or contracts are transferred to another authorized broker, entity or legal representative and approved by the Commission, the broker transferring such shall be required to compile a record of the following, retain a copy for his or her file and give a copy to the receiving authorized broker, entity or legal representative:

(A) A copy of the written approval from the Commission authorizing the transfer of the contracts and/or funds.

(B) The name and address of the authorized broker, entity or legal representative.

(C) A trust account reconciliation sheet indicating ledger balance and financial institution balance at time of transfer to include the name of each depositor, amount of deposit, date, and purpose of the deposit.

(D) A statement indicating that written agreements were obtained from all parties to each transaction agreeing to the transfer of the funds and/or contracts to another responsible broker, authorized entity or legal representative and that each depositor was notified of the effective date of transfer, and the name of the responsible person or entity.

(7) Any firm merger shall have a thirty (30) day time period in which to provide the Commission the documentation as referenced in subparagraph (n) of this rule. Firm merger means that a licensed firm has been acquired by another licensed firm and the firm that was acquired is ceasing a portion or all of its licensed activities.

(o) **Security breach of personal information.**

(1) Security breach of personal information as defined in Title 24, Oklahoma Statutes, Sections 161-166 means the unauthorized access and acquisition of unencrypted and unredacted computerized data that compromises the security or confidentiality of personal information maintained by a licensee as part of a database of personal information regarding multiple persons. Personal information means the first name or first initial and last name in combination with and linked to any one or more of the following data elements:

(A) social security number,

(B) driver license number or state identification card number issued in lieu of a driver license, or

(C) financial account number, or credit card or debit card number, in combination with any required security code, access code, or password that would permit access to the financial accounts.

(2) The breach of information would not include information that is lawfully obtained from publicly available information, or from federal, state or local government records lawfully made available to the general public.

(3) In the event personal information is breached, the licensee is required to send notice to the Commission and to all concerned persons whose information was breached by an unauthorized person or source as required in Title 24, O.S., Section 162 . The licensee is required to comply with all requirements within the Security Breach Notification Act or be subject to disciplinary action by the Commission.

605:10-13-2. Duty to account; associate

The obligation of an associate to remit monies, valuable documents and other property coming into his or her possession within the meaning of subsection six (6), Section 858-312 of the Code shall be construed to include but shall not be limited to the following:

(1) Shall turn over all documents, files and monies deposited, payments made, or things of value received by the associate to his or her broker promptly; and

(2) Shall deliver a copy of all instruments to any party or parties executing the same when such has been prepared by the associate or pertains to the consummation of a transaction in which he or she participated.

(3) Shall not be authorized to open or maintain a trust or escrow account, or be a signer on a trust or escrow account wherein the associate is providing licensed activities as defined in the License Code and Rules; however, an associate may open or maintain a trust or escrow account, or be a signer on a trust or escrow account, when the associate is performing activities as outlined in Section 858-301 of the Code.

605:10-13-3. Special escrow disbursement

(a) In the event a dispute arises prior to the disbursement of any monies or other valuables held by a broker in escrow in connection with a real estate purchase contract, the broker shall continue to retain said money or valuables in escrow until he or she has a written release from all parties consenting to its disposition or until a civil action is filed to determine its disposition at which time he or she may pay or turn it into the court.

(b) In the absence of a pending civil action and upon the passage of thirty (30) days from the date of final termination of the contract, it shall not be considered grounds for disciplinary action by the Commission against a broker for a broker to disburse escrow monies or valuables to either purchaser or seller when the disbursement has been based on a good faith decision by the broker that the opposite party has failed to perform as agreed, such disbursement to be made, however, only after fifteen (15) days written notice to all parties concerned setting forth the broker's proposed action.

605:10-15-1. Disclosure of beneficial interest or referrals

(a) No licensee shall, without disclosing such fact in writing to all parties on both sides of the transaction, either:
   (1) Accept or receive any fee, commission, salary, rebate, kickback or other compensation or consideration allowed by law in connection with the recommendation, referral or procurement of any product or service, including financial services.
   (2) Own any beneficial interest in any entity which provides any product or service, including financial services to home owners, home buyers or tenants, in connection with the sale, lease, rental or listing of any real estate. Activities or interests of associates shall ordinarily be disclosed to his or her broker who shall have the primary responsibility to make written disclosures covered by this Section to the parties.

(b) If any associate owns any beneficial interest in any entity which provides any product or service, including financial services, to home owners, home buyers, or tenants, the associate shall disclose the nature and extent of such interest to his or her broker. The obligation to make such disclosure shall be a continuing one.

(c) Notwithstanding the provisions of this Section, disclosure of a beneficial interest shall not be required if either:
   (1) The beneficial interest consists solely of a stock or other equity ownership in a publicly traded company where such ownership is less than one percent (1%) of the total equity value of such entity.
   (2) Such beneficial interest consists solely of a stock or other equity interest in a privately held company in which the aggregate ownership of all licensees employed by the firm otherwise required to make the disclosure does not exceed ten percent (10%) of the equity value of the company and where the licensee is not an officer, director, managing partner or otherwise directly or indirectly is in control of the entity which provides any product or service covered by this Section.

(d) No particular form of disclosure shall be prescribed by the Commission. All disclosures required by this Section shall be made:
   (1) Either prior to or at the time that any recommendation, referral or procurement of any product or service is made in instances in which the licensee may receive any compensation or consideration in connection therewith.
   (2) At or before the time that it becomes apparent to the licensee that any entity in which the licensee owns any beneficial interest may provide any product or service in instances in which the disclosure of any such ownership is required under this Section. All disclosures required by this Section shall be judged by the standard of whether the disclosure was adequate to inform all parties on both sides of the transaction of the existence of a beneficial interest covered by this Section or, if a party claims not to have been adequately informed, whether the form and manner in which the disclosure was made was adequate under the circumstances to inform a person of ordinary intelligence and understanding, not possessing expertise in real estate or financial matters, of the existence of any fee, compensation, salary, rebate, kickback or other compensation or consideration or the ownership of a beneficial interest in an entity providing products or services covered by this Section.

(e)   The failure by a licensee to observe any provision of this Section shall be deemed to be a violation of subsections 2, 3, 8 and 15 of Section 858-312 of the Code and in the case of an associate, a violation of subsection 4 of Section 858-312 of the Code as well.

605:10-15-2. Broker Relationships Act to become effective November 1, 2013

(a)   **Broker Relationships Act effective November 1, 2013.** A new law, Title 59, O. S., Sections 858-351 through 858-363 of the License Code, becomes effective on November 1, 2013, which law shall be referred to as the Broker Relationships Act.

(b)   **Brokerage service agreement defined.** The term "brokerage service agreement" shall mean an oral or written agreement to provide brokerage services entered into by a real estate broker and a person who is a party to a real estate transaction and shall include, but not be limited to, listing agreements, buyer broker agreements and property management agreements.

(c)   **Validity of a brokerage service agreement existing before and on November 1, 2013.** A brokerage service agreement entered into prior to November 1, 2013, shall remain in full force and effect until the agreement expires or is otherwise terminated by an agreement of the parties.

(d)   **Providing services to more than one party to the transaction.** When a firm provides brokerage services to more than one party to the transaction, the broker shall provide written notice to those parties that the broker is providing brokerage services to more than one party. When a firm provides brokerage services to both sides of the transaction, the firm shall ensure compliance with the duties and responsibilities in Title 59, O.S., Section 858-353 along with all other requirements of the License Code and Rules.

(e)   **Services provided to a tenant.** When a broker provides brokerage services to a landlord under a property management agreement, the services provided to the tenant by the broker shall not be construed as creating a broker relationship between the broker and the tenant unless otherwise agreed to in writing; however, the broker owes to the tenant the duties of honesty and exercising reasonable skill and care.

605:10-15-3. Requirements for furnishing psychological factors

Psychologically impacted property is any property where the existence of certain circumstances, suspicions or facts may create emotional or psychological disturbance or concerns to a prospective purchaser/lessee, with the potential of influencing a buying/leasing decision. Therefore, the obligation of a real estate licensee to obtain information as stated in Title 59, O.S., Section 858-513A (1) and (2) shall be performed in the following manner:

(1)   Purchaser/lessee must be in the process of making a bona fide offer.

(2)   Licensee must receive request in writing from purchaser/lessee.

(3)   Purchaser's/Lessee's written request must state that such factor is important to the decision of the purchaser/lessee.

(4)   Licensee shall make inquiry of the owner by submitting the written request to the owner.

(5)   Licensee shall report any findings to the purchaser/lessee with the consent of the owner.

(6)   If the owner refuses to furnish information requested, the licensee shall so advise the purchaser/lessee.

(7)   Further, if a purchaser/lessee is requesting information as to whether or not an occupant of the real estate is, or was at any time suspected to be infected, or has been infected with Acquired Immune Deficiency Syndrome, or any other disease which falls under the privacy laws, the information can only be obtained in accordance with the Public Health and Safety Statute, Title 63, O.S., 1988, Section 1-502.2A.

605:10-15-4. Residential Property Condition Disclosure Act forms

(a)   **Development and amendment of forms.** In accordance with Oklahoma Statutes, Title 60, Section 833 the Commission shall develop and amend by rule the forms for the Residential Property Condition Disclosure Statement and Residential Property Condition Disclaimer Statement. Effective July 11, 2008 the disclosure statement is amended and all disclosure forms executed prior to July 11, 2008 will remain in force and valid until expiration of the 180 days from the date noted thereon.

(b)   **Availability of forms.** The forms shall be available to the public upon request on and after July 1, 1995.

(c)   **Copy of form format.** The Residential Property Condition Disclosure Statement as referenced in this section is set out in Appendix A at the end of this Chapter. The Residential Property Condition Disclaimer Statement as referenced in this section is set out in Appendix B at the end of this Chapter.

605:10-17-1. Commissions and disputes

(a) The Commission shall not establish the rate of commissions to be charged for real estate services and shall have no interest therein.

(b) At its discretion, the Commission may dismiss or postpone any investigation or hearing which essentially involves a dispute not affecting the public interest until or unless such dispute is resolved.

(c) The Commission shall entertain a complaint against a broker charging a violation of subsection 18 of Section 858-312 of this "Code" only if the complaining licensee submits with his or her complaint evidence that a court of competent jurisdiction has ruled in his or her favor relative to the subject and awarded judgment against the broker.

605:10-17-2. Complaint procedures

(a) **Complaint may be filed by public or Commission's own motion.** A complaint alleging misconduct on the part of a licensee or any person unlicensed pursuant to the Code who violates provisions of the Code may be filed by any person in writing on a form for such supplied by the Commission, or may be ordered by the Commission on its own motion. The Commission will accept a complaint alleging misconduct on a form not supplied by the Commission if such form is notarized by a notary public.

(b) **Complaint notification; licensee response.** When a complaint has been filed the licensee or unlicensed person pursuant to the Code shall be immediately notified and shall be required to file an adequate written response within fifteen (15) days of the notice.

(c) **Investigation and/or investigative session.** Subsequent to the fifteen (15) day answer period, a field investigation or preliminary investigative session may be conducted to ascertain whether or not charges should be lodged and a formal hearing ordered. Such investigation or investigative session shall be under the supervision of the Secretary-Treasurer of the Commission. He or she may designate an attorney who will act as prosecutor for the Commission to examine the results of the field investigation and/or conduct a preliminary investigative session. The prosecutor so designated may in the name of the Commission subpoena witnesses, take testimony by deposition and compel the production of records and documents bearing upon the complaint.

(d) **Findings reported to Commission.** At the completion of the investigation or investigative session, a written report accompanied by findings, if any, shall be submitted to the Commission. Following receipt of the report, the Commission shall determine whether or not the apparent evidence warrants lodging formal charges and ordering a formal hearing, and if a formal hearing is ordered all parties shall then be furnished with copies of any written report accompanied by findings, if any.

605:10-17-3. Complaint hearings; notice and procedures

(a) **Summary suspension.** If the Commission finds that public health, safety, or welfare imperatively requires emergency action, and incorporates a finding to that effect in its order, summary suspension of a license may be ordered pending proceedings for revocation or other action within thirty (30) days. The summary suspension shall remain in effect until further order by the Commission.

(b) **Formal hearing ordered; notification.** Except as provided in (a) of this section, the Commission may issue a disciplinary order only after a hearing of which licensee or unlicensed person pursuant to the Code affected shall be given at least fifteen (15) days written notice, specifying the offenses of which the licensee or unlicensed person pursuant to the Code is charged. Such notice may be served as provided by law for service of notices, or by mailing a copy by certified mail to the last known address. If the licensee is an associate associated with a broker, the Commission in like manner shall notify the broker with whom associated.

(c) **Formal hearing location.** The hearing on such charges shall be set at such time and place as the Commission through its Secretary-Treasurer may prescribe and the notice in (b) of this section shall specify this time and place.

(d) **Formal hearing before Commission; hearing examiner or selected panel.** The Secretary-Treasurer shall schedule each formal disciplinary hearing before a Hearing Examiner, a selected panel of the Commission, or the Commission as a whole. In the case of a proceeding conducted by the Commission as a whole or a panel of the Commission, the Chairman or his/her designee shall preside. Designated counsel shall advise the Chair as to rulings upon the questions of admissibility of evidence, competence of witnesses and any other question of law where such ruling is required or requested.

(e) **Request for postponement.** Once a hearing has been scheduled, the Secretary-Treasurer may for sufficient cause postpone or reschedule a hearing upon proper motion or request having been filed with the Commission office seventy-two (72) hours prior to the hearing.

    (1) Each postponement request must be in writing and must state the specific reason(s) for the request.

    (2) The Commission may require official documentation supporting such request.

    (3) An emergency postponement request shall be considered at the time of the emergency.

    (4) The granting of a continuance whether general or emergency, shall not be interpreted to deny the Commission the power to impose summary suspension if the Commission finds that public health, safety, or welfare imperatively requires emergency action, and incorporates a finding to that effect in its Order, summary suspension of a license may be ordered pending proceedings for revocation or other action within thirty (30) days.

(f) **Hearings public; witnesses may be excluded.** All hearings shall be public except that upon motion of either party, witnesses may be excluded from the hearing room when such witness is not testifying.

(g) **Court reporter.** A court reporter shall be present to record the proceedings on behalf of the Commission. Any person desiring a copy of the transcript of the proceedings, may purchase such from the reporter.

(h) **Formal hearing procedures.** The designated attorney for the State shall present the State's case. The respondent may present his or her own evidence or may present such through his or her own counsel. If the charges against the respondent resulted from a complaint filed by a party present at the hearing, the complaining party may be a witness for the State. In order that the hearing will not be encumbered by evidence having no bearing on the issues, testimony by all witnesses will be limited to matters relevant to the issues involved. The order of procedure shall be as follows:

    (1) Recitation of the statement of charges by the person presiding.

    (2) Opening statement by the State.

    (3) Opening statement by the respondent.

    (4) Presentation of the State's case followed by cross-examination and questioning by the Hearing Examiner or Hearing panel.

    (5) Respondent's presentation followed by cross-examination and questioning by the Hearing Examiner or Hearing panel.

    (6) Closing arguments by the State.

    (7) Closing arguments by the respondent.

(i) **Order; hearing before commission.** If the case be heard by the Commission as a whole, the Commission shall deliberate and render a decision with confirmation of such decision in writing in the form of an Order distributed to all parties by mail.

(j) **Proposed order consideration; hearing before hearing examiner or panel.** In the case of a hearing conducted by a panel of the Commission or by a Hearing Examiner, following the hearing, the Hearing Examiner or attorney sitting as counsel to the panel shall prepare a proposed Order to be considered by members of the Real Estate Commission at a future meeting.

(k) **Proposed order notification; written exceptions.** Affected parties will be furnished copies of the proposed Order and notified as to the date the proposal will be considered by the Commission for adoption. At the same time, notice will also be given to the parties that written exceptions or requests to present oral exceptions or arguments, if any, should be submitted on or before a designated date pursuant to Section 311, of Title 75, Oklahoma Statutes. Upon adoption of the Order by the Commission as a whole, the adopted Order shall be distributed to all parties.

(l) **Actual notification pertaining to this Section.** For purposes of this Section, notice shall be deemed to have been given at the time that notice is deposited in the United States mail with proper postage thereon and mailed to the last known address of the notified person, or date when such notice is served in person by a person duly authorized as a representative of the Commission.

(m) **Violation found.** If the Commission shall determine that any licensee or unlicensed person pursuant to the Code is guilty of violation of the "Code," such person may be disciplined in the manner as prescribed in such "Code."

605:10-17-4. Prohibited dealings

Within the meaning of subsection 8 of Section 858-312 of the "Code," untrustworthy, improper, fraudulent or dishonest dealing shall include, but not be limited to, the following:

    (1) The making of a brokerage service contract without a date of termination.

(2) Purchasing of property by a licensee for himself or herself or another entity in which the licensee has an interest as defined in 605:10-15-1 (c), if such property is listed with the broker or the broker's firm, without first making full disclosure thereof and obtaining the approval of the owner, or the failure by the licensee to exert the licensee's best effort in order to later purchase or acquire the property for themself or another entity in which they have an interest as defined in 605:10-15-1 (c).

(3) Repeated misrepresentations, even though not fraudulent, which occur as a result of the failure by the licensee to inform himself or herself of pertinent facts concerning property, as to which he or she is performing services.

(4) Procuring the signature to a purchase offer or contract or to any lease or lease proposal which has no definite purchase price or lease rental, or no method of payment, termination date, possession date or property description.

(5) The payment of any fees or amounts due the Commission with a check that is dishonored upon presentation to the bank on which the check is drawn.

(6) Lending a broker's license to an associate; permitting an associate to operate as a broker; or failure of a broker to properly supervise the activities of an associate. A broker permitting the use of the broker's license to enable an associate licensed with the broker to, in fact, establish and conduct a brokerage business wherein the broker's only interest is the receipt of a fee for the use of the broker's sponsorship.

(7) Failure to make known in writing to any purchaser any interest the licensee has in the property they are selling.

(8) Failure of the licensee to inform the buyer and seller in writing at the time the offer is presented that the buyer and seller will be expected to pay certain closing costs, such as discount points and approximate amount of said costs.

(9) Failing, upon demand in writing, to respond to a complaint in writing, or to disclose any information within licensee's knowledge, or to produce any document, book or record in licensee's possession or under licensee's control that is real estate related and under the jurisdiction of the Real Estate Commission, for inspection to a member of the Commission staff or any other lawful representative of the Commission.

(10) Failure to reduce a bona fide offer to writing, where a proposed purchaser requests such offer to be submitted.

(11) Failure to submit all written bona fide offers to an owner when such offers are received prior to the seller accepting an offer in writing.

(12) Any conduct in a real estate transaction which demonstrates bad faith or incompetency.

(13) Failing to act, in marketing a licensee's own property, with the same good faith as when acting in the capacity of a real estate licensee.

(14) An associate who does not possess the license of a broker or branch office broker but is intentionally acting in the capacity of a broker or branch office broker.

(15) Discouraging a party from obtaining an inspection on a property.

(16) Allowing access to, or control of, real property without the owner's authorization.

(17) Knowingly providing false or misleading information to the Commission during the course of an investigation.

(18) Interfering with an investigation by means of persuading, intimidating or threatening any party or witness, or tampering with or withholding evidence relating to the investigation.

(19) Knowingly cooperating with an unlicensed person or entity to perform licensed real estate activities as required by Title 59 O.S. Section 858-301.

(20) Failing to disclose any known immediate family relationship to a party to the transaction for which the broker is providing brokerage services.

(21) Failure by a broker to ensure all persons performing real estate licensed activities under the broker are properly licensed.

(22) An associate shall not perform licensed activities outside their broker's supervision.

(23) Failing to maintain documents relating to a trust account or real estate transaction for the time period as required by Rule 605:10-13-1.

605:10-17-5. Substantial misrepresentation

Substantial misrepresentation within the meaning of paragraph 2 of Section 858-312 of the "Code" includes, but is not limited to:

(1) The recommendation or use by a licensee of a fictitious or false instrument for the purpose of inducing any lender or Government Agency to loan or insure any sum of money.

(2) Failure to disclose to a buyer or other cooperative licensee or firm a known material defect regarding the condition of a parcel of real estate of which a broker or associate has knowledge.

(3) The use by a real estate broker of the name or trade name of a licensee whose license has been revoked or currently on suspension.

(4) Representing to any lender, guaranteeing agency or any other interested party, either verbally or through the preparation of false documents, an amount in excess of the true and actual sales price of the real property or terms differing from those actually agreed upon by the parties to the transaction.

605:10-17-6. Requirements for suspended/revoked licensee

(a) A suspended/revoked licensee must return their license certificate and pocket identification card to the Commission office on or before the date the suspension/revocation becomes effective.

(b) When the suspension/revocation period becomes effective, the licensee shall comply with the following requirements:

(1) A suspended/revoked licensee shall not engage in any activity which requires a real estate license, as defined in Section 858-102.

(2) When a broker's license is suspended/revoked, associates under the suspended/revoked broker's supervision will automatically be placed "inactive" for the duration of the suspension/revocation period unless the licensee requests to be transferred to another broker.

(3) If the suspended/revoked broker has a branch office, the license for the branch office will be placed inactive unless otherwise ordered by the Commission; and all licensees associated with the branch office will automatically be placed "inactive" for the duration of the suspension/revocation period unless the licensee requests to be transferred to another broker.

(4) If a managing corporate broker of a corporation is suspended/revoked for an act which was on behalf of the corporation, the broker license of the corporation will be placed inactive unless otherwise ordered by the Commission; and all licensees associated with the corporation will automatically be placed "inactive" for the duration of the suspension/revocation period unless the licensee requests to be transferred to another broker.

(5) If the managing partner(s) of a partnership is suspended/revoked for an act which was in behalf of the partnership, the broker license of the partnership will be placed inactive unless otherwise ordered by the Commission; and all licensees associated with the partnership will automatically be placed on "inactive" for the duration of the suspension/revocation period and the other broker will be placed "inactive" unless he or she requests his or her license to be transferred out of the partnership.

(6) If a managing broker member of an association is suspended/revoked for an act which was in behalf of the association, the broker license of the association will be placed inactive unless otherwise ordered by the Commission; and all licensees associated with the association will automatically be placed "inactive" for the duration of the suspension/revocation period unless the licensee requests to be transferred to another broker.

(7) A suspended/revoked licensee shall only receive compensation during the suspension/revocation period for acts which were performed during the period in which the licensee was actively licensed.

(8) Listings must be cancelled by a suspended/revoked broker between the time the Order of suspension/revocation is received and the effective date of suspension/revocation, as listings will be void on the date the suspension/revocation becomes effective.

(9) A suspended/revoked broker shall not assign listings to another broker without the written consent of the owner of the listed property.

(10) A suspended/revoked broker shall not advertise real estate in any manner, and must remove and discontinue all advertising.

(11) The telephone in a suspended/revoked broker's office shall not be answered in any manner to indicate the suspended/revoked broker is currently active in real estate.

(12) All pending contracts, items or monies placed with the suspended/revoked broker must be transferred to another responsible broker as approved by the Commission and in compliance with Section 605:10-13-1 (n).

(13) A suspended/revoked licensee shall be required to comply with Section 605:10-13-1 (n) and provide the required information to the Commission prior to the effective date of suspension/revocation.

(14) A representative of the Commission shall visit the office of any suspended/revoked broker prior to the effective date of the suspension/revocation to insure compliance with the requirements of (1) through (13) of this subsection.

605:10-17-7. Cessation of licensed activities upon loss of license

(a) A revoked, suspended, cancelled, surrendered or lapsed licensee is prohibited from performing licensed activities upon the effective date of loss of license.

(b) A revoked or suspended licensee shall comply with Section 605:10-17-6.

(c) A broker whose license was cancelled, surrendered or lapsed shall comply with Section 605:10-13-1 (m.)

APPENDIX A. RESIDENTIAL PROPERTY CONDITION DISCLOSURE STATEMENT

Notice to Seller: Oklahoma Law (the "Residential Property Condition Disclosure Act," Title 60, O.S., §831 et.seq., effective July 1, 1995) requires Sellers of 1 and/or 2 residential dwelling units to complete this form. A Seller must complete, sign and date this disclosure form and deliver it or cause it to be delivered to a purchaser as soon as practicable, but in any event no later than before an offer is accepted by the Seller. If the Seller becomes aware of a defect after delivery of this statement, but before the Seller accepts an offer to purchase, the Seller must deliver or cause to be delivered an amended disclosure statement disclosing the newly discovered defect to the Purchaser. If the disclosure form or amendment is delivered to a Purchaser after an offer to purchase has been made by the Purchaser, the offer to purchase shall be accepted by the Seller only after a Purchaser has acknowledged receipt of this statement and confirmed the offer to purchase in writing.

Notice to Purchaser: The declarations and information contained in this disclosure statement are not warranties, express or implied of any kind, and are not a substitute for any inspections or warranties the Purchaser may wish to obtain. The information contained in this disclosure statement is not intended to be a part of any contract between the Purchaser and Seller. The information and statements contained in this disclosure statement are declarations and representations of the Seller and are not the representations of the real estate licensee.

LOCATION OF SUBJECT PROPERTY_____

_____

SELLER IS ___ IS NOT ___ OCCUPYING THE SUBJECT PROPERTY.

Instructions to the Seller: (1) Answer ALL questions. (2) Report known conditions affecting the property. (3) Complete this form yourself. (4) If an item is not on the property, or will not be included in the sale, mark "None/Not Included." If you do not know the facts, mark "Do Not Know if Working." (5) The date of completion by you may not be more than 180 days prior to the date this form is received by a purchaser.

ARE THE ITEMS LISTED BELOW IN NORMAL WORKING ORDER?

Appliances/Systems/ Services	Working	Not Working	Do Not Know if Working	None/ Not Included
Sprinkler System				
Swimming Pool				
Hot Tub/Spa				
Water Heater ___ Electric ___ Gas ___ Solar				
Water Purifier				
Water Softener ___ Leased ___ Owned				
Sump Pump				
Plumbing				
Whirlpool Tub				
Sewer System ___ Public ___ Septic ___ Lagoon				
Air Conditioning System ___ Electric ___ Gas ___ Heat Pump				
Window Air Conditioner(s)				
Attic Fan				
Fireplaces				
Heating System ___ Electric ___ Gas ___ Heat Pump				
Humidifier				
Ceiling Fans				

Appliances/Systems/ Services	Working	Not Working	Do Not Know if Working	None/ Not Included
Gas Supply ___ Public ___ Propane ___ Butane				
Propane Tank ___ Leased ___ Owned				
Electric Air Purifier				
Garage Door Opener				
Intercom				
Central Vacuum				
Security System ___ Rent ___ Own ___ Monitored				
Smoke Detectors				
Dishwasher				
Electrical Wiring				
Garbage Disposal				
Gas Grill				
Vent Hood				
Microwave Oven				
Built-in Oven/Range				
Kitchen Stove				
Trash Compactor				
Source of Household Water ___ Public ___ Well ___ Private/Rural District				

Buyer's Initials _____ Buyer's Initials _____   Seller's Initials _____ Seller's Initials _____

(OREC—11/17)   Page 1 of 3

LOCATION OF SUBJECT PROPERTY_____

IF YOU ANSWERED Not Working to any items on page one, please explain. Attach additional pages with your signature.

Zoning and Historical		
1. Property is zoned: (Check One) ___ residential ____ commercial ____ historical ___ office ___ agricultural ___ industrial ___ urban conservation ___ other ___ unknown		
2. Is the property designated as historical or located in a registered historical district? Yes _____ No _____		

Flood and Water	Yes	No
3. What is the flood zone status of the property? _____		
4. Are you aware if the property is located in a floodway as defined in the Oklahoma Floodplain Management Act?		
5. Are you aware of any flood insurance requirements concerning the property?		
6. Are you aware of any flood insurance on the property?		
7. Are you aware of the property being damaged or affected by flood, storm run-off, sewer backup, draining or grading problems?		
8. Are you aware of any surface or ground water drainage systems which assist in draining the property, e.g. "French Drains?"		
9. Are you aware of any occurrence of water in the heating and air conditioning duct system?		
10. Are you aware of water seepage, leakage or other draining problems in any of the improvements on the property?		

Additions/Alterations/Repairs	Yes	No
11. Are you aware of any additions being made without required permits?		
12. Are you aware of any previous foundation repairs?		
13. Are you aware of any alterations or repairs having been made to correct defects or problems?		
14. Are you aware of any defect or condition affecting the interior or exterior walls, ceilings, roof structure, slab/foundation, basement/storm cellar, floors, windows, doors, fences or garage?		
15. Are you aware of the roof covering ever being repaired or replaced during your ownership of the property?		
16. Approximate age of roof covering, if known _____ number of layers, if known _____		
17. Do you know of any current problems with the roof covering?		
18. Are you aware of treatment for termite or wood-destroying organism infestation?		
19. Are you aware of a termite bait system installed on the property?		
20. If yes, is it being monitored by a licensed exterminating company? If yes, annual cost $_____		
21. Are you aware of any damage caused by termites or wood-destroying organisms?		
22. Are you aware of major fire, tornado, hail, earthquake or wind damage?		
23. Have you ever received payment on an insurance claim for damages to residential property and/or any improvements which were not repaired?		
24. Are you aware of problems pertaining to sewer, septic, lateral lines or aerobic system?		

Environmental (Continued on Page 3)	Yes	No
25. Are you aware of the presence of asbestos?		
26. Are you aware of the presence of radon gas?		
27. Have you tested for radon gas?		
28. Are you aware of the presence of lead-based paint?		
29. Have you tested for lead-based paint?		
30. Are you aware of any underground storage tanks on the property?		
31. Are you aware of the presence of a landfill on the property?		
32. Are you aware of the existence of hazardous or regulated materials and other conditions having an environmental impact?		
33. Are you aware of the existence of prior manufacturing of methamphetamine?		
34. Have you had the property inspected for mold?		
35. Are you aware of any remedial treatment for mold on the property?		
36. Are you aware of any condition on the property that would impair the health or safety of the occupants?		

Buyer's Initials _____   Buyer's Initials _____   Seller's Initials _____ Seller's Initials _____

Oklahoma Real Estate Commission Rules

LOCATION OF SUBJECT PROPERTY_____		

Environmental (Continued from Page 2)	Yes	No
37. Are you aware of any wells located on the property?		
38. Are you aware of any dams located on the property? If yes, are you responsible for the maintenance of that dam? _____ YES _____ NO		

Property Shared in Common, Easements, Homeowner's Associations and Legal	Yes	No
39. Are you aware of features of the property shared in common with the adjoining landowners, such as fences, driveways, and roads whose use or responsibility has an effect on the property?		
40. Other than utility easements serving the property, are you aware of any easements or right-of-ways affecting the property?		
41. Are you aware of encroachments affecting the property?		
42. Are you aware of a mandatory homeowner's association? Amount of dues $_____ Special Assessment $_____ Payable: (check one) _____ monthly _____ quarterly _____ annually Are there unpaid dues or assessments for the property? _____ YES _____ NO If yes, what is the amount? $_____ Manager's Name _____ Phone Number _____		
43. Are you aware of any zoning, building code or setback requirement violations?		
44. Are you aware of any notices from any government or government-sponsored agencies or any other entities affecting the property?		
45. Are you aware of any surface leases, including but not limited to agricultural, commercial or oil and gas?		
46. Are you aware of any filed litigation or lawsuits directly or indirectly affecting the property, including a foreclosure?		
47. Is the property located in a fire district which requires payment? If yes, amount of fee $_____ Paid to Whom _____ Payable: (check one) _____ monthly _____ quarterly _____ annually		
48. Is the property located in a private utility district? Check applicable _____ Water _____ Garbage _____ Sewer _____ Other If other, explain _____ Initial membership fee $_____ Annual membership fee $_____ (if more than one utility attach additional pages)		

Miscellaneous	Yes	No
49. Are you aware of other defect(s) affecting the property not disclosed above?		
50. Are you aware of any other fees or dues required on the property that you have not disclosed?		

If you answered YES to any of the items on pages two and three, list the item number(s) and explain. If needed, attach additional pages with your signature(s), date(s) and location of the subject property. _____
_____
_____

On the date this form is signed, the seller states that based on seller's **CURRENT ACTUAL KNOWLEDGE** of the property, the information contained above is true and accurate.

Are there any additional pages attached to this disclosure? (circle one): YES   NO   If yes, how many? _____

_____   _____   _____   _____
Seller's Signature   Date   Seller's Signature   Date

A real estate licensee has no duty to the Seller or the Purchaser to conduct an independent inspection of the property and has no duty to independently verify the accuracy or completeness of any statement made by the Seller in the disclosure statement.

The Purchaser understands that the disclosures given by the Seller on this statement are not a warranty of condition. The Purchaser is urged to carefully inspect the property, and, if desired, to have the property inspected by a licensed expert. For specific uses, restrictions and flood zone status, contact the local planning, zoning and/or engineering department. The Purchaser acknowledges that the Purchaser has read and received a signed copy of this statement. This completed acknowledgement should accompany an offer to purchase on the property identified. This is to advise that this disclosure statement is not valid after 180 days from the date completed by the Seller.

_____   _____   _____   _____
Purchaser's Signature   Date   Purchaser's Signature   Date

The disclosure and disclaimer statement forms and the Oklahoma Residential Property Condition Disclosure Act information pamphlet are made available at the Oklahoma Real Estate Commission (OREC), Denver N. Davison Building, 1915 N. Stiles, Suite 200, Oklahoma City, OK 73105, or visit OREC's Web site www.orec.ok.gov.

(OREC—11/17)   Page 3 of 3

APPENDIX B. RESIDENTIAL PROPERTY CONDITION DISCLAIMER STATEMENT FORM

Seller instructions: Oklahoma Law (the "Residential Property Condition Disclosure Act," 60, O.S. Section 831 et. seq., effective July 1, 1995) **requires a seller** of 1 and 2 residential dwelling units **to deliver, or cause to be delivered, a disclaimer statement to a purchaser as soon as practicable, but in any event before acceptance of an offer to purchase if you, the seller: 1) have never occupied the property and make no disclosures** concerning the condition of the property; <u>and</u> **2) have no actual knowledge of any defect** concerning the property.

If, however, you occupied the property or **know of a defect in regard to the property,** you must complete and deliver, or cause to be delivered, a "Residential Property Condition Disclosure Statement" to the purchaser.

Also, if you become aware of a defect <u>after</u> delivery of this disclaimer statement to a purchaser, but before you accept an offer to purchase, you must complete and deliver, or cause to be delivered, a "Residential Property Condition Disclosure Statement" to a purchaser.

Completion of this form by you **may not be more than 180 days prior to the date this form is received by a purchaser.**

Note: If this disclaimer statement **is delivered to a purchaser after an offer to purchase has been made by the purchaser,** the offer to purchase **shall be accepted by you only after** a purchaser has acknowledged receipt of this statement and confirmed the offer to purchase.

> Defect means a condition, malfunction, or problem that would have a materially adverse effect on the monetary value of the property, or that would impair the health or safety of future occupants of the property.

(For more information on the requirements of the law, please refer to the Residential Property Condition Disclosure Information Pamphlet.)

Seller's Disclaimer Statement

The undersigned seller states that seller has <u>never</u> occupied the property located at _____ _____, Oklahoma; makes <u>no</u> disclosures concerning the condition of the property; AND has <u>no</u> actual knowledge of any defect.

Seller's Signature	Date	Seller's Signature	Date

Purchaser's Acknowledgment

The purchaser shall sign and date this acknowledgment. The purchaser is urged to carefully inspect the subject property and, if desired, to have the property inspected by an expert. The purchaser acknowledges that purchaser has read and received a signed copy of this statement. This completed acknowledgement should accompany an offer to purchase you make on the property identified above.

Purchaser's Signature	Date	Purchaser's Signature	Date

Note to seller and purchaser: A real estate licensee has no duty to the seller or purchaser to conduct an independent inspection of the property and has no duty to independently verify the accuracy or completeness of any statement made by the seller in this disclaimer statement.

The disclosure and disclaimer statement forms and the Residential Property Condition Disclosure Information Pamphlet are made available by the Oklahoma Real Estate Commission, 1915 N. Stiles Ave., Suite 200 (Denver N. Davison Building), Oklahoma City, Oklahoma 73105-4919. Visit the Commission's web site: www.orec.ok.gov

OREC (07-2014)

Residential Property Condition Disclosure Act

Title 60. Chapter 16A - Residential Property Condition Disclosure Act

§831. Short Title

This act shall be known and may be cited as the "Residential Property Condition Disclosure Act".

§832. Definitions

As used in this act:
1. "Offer to purchase" means an offer to purchase property made by a purchaser pursuant to a written contract;
2. "Seller" means one or more persons who are attempting to transfer a possessory interest in property and who are either:
3. represented by a real estate licensee; or
4. not represented by a real estate licensee but receive a written request from the purchaser to deliver or cause to be delivered a disclaimer statement or disclosure statement as such terms are defined in paragraphs 11 and 12 of this section;
5. "Purchaser" means one or more persons who are attempting to acquire a possessory interest in property;
6. "Real estate licensee" means a person licensed under the Oklahoma Real Estate License Code;
7. "Transfer" means a sale or conveyance, exchange or option to purchase by written instrument of a possessory interest in property for consideration;
8. "Person" means an individual, corporation, limited liability company, partnership, association, trust or other legal entity or any combination thereof;
9. "Contract" means a real estate purchase contract for the sale, conveyance or exchange of property, option to purchase property, or a lease with an option to purchase property;
10. "Property" means residential real property improved with not less than one nor more than two dwelling units;
11. "Defect" means a condition, malfunction or problem that would have a materially adverse effect on the monetary value of the property, or that would impair the health or safety of future occupants of the property;
12. "Disclosure" means a written declaration required by this act based on actual knowledge of the seller regarding certain physical conditions of the property. A disclosure for purposes of this act is not a warranty, implied or express, of any kind;
13. "Disclaimer statement" means the statement described in paragraph 1 of subsection A of Section 3 of this act; and
14. "Disclosure statement" means the statement described in paragraph 2 of subsection A of Section 3 of this act.

§833. Property Disclaimer or Disclosure Statement

(A) A seller of property located in this state shall deliver, or cause to be delivered, to the purchaser of such property one of the following:
  (1) A written property disclaimer statement on a form established by rule by the Oklahoma Real Estate Commission which states that the seller:
    (a) has never occupied the property and makes no disclosures concerning the condition of the property, and
    (b) has no actual knowledge of any defect; or

(2) A written property condition disclosure statement on a form established by rule by the Oklahoma Real Estate Commission which shall include the information set forth in subsection B of this section.

(B) 1. The disclosure statement shall include an identification of items and improvements which are included in the sale of the property and whether such items or improvements are in normal working order. The disclosures required shall also include a statement of whether the seller has actual knowledge of defects or information in relation to the following:

    (a) water and sewer systems, including the source of household water, water treatment systems, sprinkler systems, occurrence of water in the heating and air conditioning ducts, water seepage or leakage, drainage or grading problems and flood zone status,

    (b) structural systems, including the roof, walls, floors, foundation and any basement,

    (c) plumbing, electrical, heating and air conditioning systems,

    (d) infestation or damage of wood-destroying organisms,

    (e) major fire or tornado damage,

    (f) land use matters,

    (g) existence of hazardous or regulated materials and other conditions having an environmental impact,

    (h) existence of prior manufacturing of methamphetamine,

    (i) any other defects known to the seller, and

    (j) other matters the Oklahoma Real Estate Commission deems appropriate.

(2) The disclosure statement shall include the following notices to the purchaser in bold and conspicuous type:

    (a) "The information and statements contained in this disclosure statement are declarations and representations of the seller and are not the representations of the real estate licensee.",

    (b) "The information contained in this disclosure statement is not intended to be a part of any contract between the purchaser and the seller.", and

    (c) "The declarations and information contained in this disclosure statement are not warranties, express or implied of any kind, and are not a substitute for any inspections or warranties the purchaser may wish to obtain."

(C) Either the disclaimer statement or the disclosure statement required by this section must be completed, signed and dated by the seller. The date of completion on either statement may not be more than one hundred eighty (180) days prior to the date of receipt of the statement by the purchaser.

(D) The Oklahoma Real Estate Commission shall develop by rule the forms for the residential property condition disclaimer and the residential property condition disclosure statement. After development of the initial forms, the Oklahoma Real Estate Commission may amend by rule the forms as is necessary and appropriate.

(E) Such forms shall be made available upon request irrespective of whether the person requesting a disclaimer or disclosure form is represented by a real estate licensee.

§834. Delivery of Disclaimer or Disclosure Statement

A. A seller should deliver either the disclaimer statement or disclosure statement to the purchaser as soon as practicable, but in any event it shall be delivered before acceptance of an offer to purchase.

B. If the disclaimer statement or disclosure statement is delivered to the purchaser after an offer to purchase has been made, the offer to purchase shall be accepted only after the purchaser has acknowledged receipt of the disclaimer statement or disclosure statement and confirmed the offer to purchase.

C. If the seller becomes aware of a defect after delivery to the purchaser of either a disclaimer statement or a disclosure statement, then the seller shall promptly deliver to the purchaser either a disclosure statement or an amended disclosure statement which discloses the newly discovered defect. The disclosure statement or any amendment shall be in writing and shall be signed and dated by the seller. However, if the required document is delivered to the purchaser after an offer to purchase has been made, the offer to purchase shall be accepted only after the purchaser has acknowledged receipt of the required document and confirmed the offer to purchase.

D. The purchaser shall acknowledge in writing receipt of the disclaimer statement or the disclosure statement and any amendment to the disclosure statement. The purchaser shall sign and date any acknowledgment. Such acknowledgment should accompany the offer to purchase the property. If the purchaser confirms the offer to purchase, such confirmation shall be in writing, shall be signed and dated by the purchaser and shall be promptly delivered to the seller.

§835. Liability of Seller

A. The seller shall not be liable for a defect or other condition in the property if the existence of the defect or other condition in the property was disclosed in the disclosure statement or any amendment delivered to the purchaser before acceptance of the offer to purchase.

B. The seller shall not be liable for any erroneous, inaccurate or omitted information supplied to the purchaser as a disclosure required by this act if:
1. The error, inaccuracy or omission results from an approximation of information by the seller, provided:
    a. accurate information was unknown to the seller at the time the disclosure was made,
    b. the approximation was clearly identified as such and was reasonable and based on the best information available to the seller, and
    c. the approximation was not used to circumvent the disclosure requirements of this act;
2. The error, inaccuracy or omission was not within the actual knowledge of the seller; or
3. The disclosure was based on information provided by public agencies and the seller reasonably believed the information to be correct.

C. The delivery by a public agency of any information required to be disclosed by the seller of the property shall satisfy the requirements of this act as to the disclosures to which the information being furnished is applicable.

§836. Duties of Real Estate Licensee Representing or Assisting Seller or Purchaser

A. A real estate licensee representing or assisting a seller has the duty to obtain from the seller a disclaimer statement or a disclosure statement and any amendment required by the Residential Property Condition Disclosure Act and to make such statement available to potential purchasers prior to acceptance of an offer to purchase.

B. A real estate licensee representing or assisting a purchaser has the duty to obtain and make available to the purchaser a disclaimer statement or a disclosure statement and any amendment required by the Residential Property Condition Disclosure Act prior to the acceptance of an offer to purchase.

C. A real estate licensee has the duty to disclose to the purchaser any defects in the property actually known to the licensee which are not included in the disclosure statement or any amendment.

D. A real estate licensee who has complied with the requirements of subsections A, B and C of this section, as applicable, shall have no further duties to the seller or the purchaser regarding any disclosures required under the Residential Property Condition Disclosure Act.

A real estate licensee who has not complied with the requirements of subsections A, B and C of this section shall be subject to disciplinary action by the Oklahoma Real Estate Commission as set forth in paragraph 6 of Section 858-208 of Title 59 of the Oklahoma Statutes.

E. A real estate licensee has no duty to the seller or the purchaser to conduct an independent inspection of the property and has no duty to independently verify the accuracy or completeness of any statement made by the seller in the disclaimer statement or the disclosure statement and any amendment.

§837. Remedies - Recovery by Purchaser

A. The purchaser may recover in a civil action only in the event of any of the following:
1. The failure of the seller to provide to the purchaser a disclaimer statement or a disclosure statement and any amendment prior to acceptance of an offer to purchase;
2. The failure of the seller to disclose in the disclosure statement or any amendment provided to the purchaser a defect which was actually known to the seller prior to acceptance of an offer to purchase; or
3. The failure of the real estate licensee to disclose to the purchaser any defects in the property actually known to the real estate licensee prior to acceptance of an offer to purchase and which were not included in the disclosure statement or any amendment provided to the purchaser.

B. The sole and exclusive civil remedy at common law or otherwise for a failure under subsection A of this section by the seller or the real estate licensee shall be an action for actual damages, including the cost of repairing the defect, suffered by the purchaser as a result of a defect existing in the property as of the date of acceptance by the seller of an offer to purchase and shall not include the remedy of exemplary damages.

C.   Any action brought under this act shall be commenced within two (2) years after the date of transfer of real property subject to this act.

D.   In any civil action brought under this act, the prevailing party shall be allowed court costs and a reasonable attorney fee to be set by the court and to be collected as costs.

E.   A transfer of a possessory interest in property subject to this act may not be invalidated solely because of the failure of any person to comply with this act.

F.   This act applies to, regulates and determines rights, duties, obligations and remedies at common law or otherwise of the seller, the real estate licensee and the purchaser with respect to disclosure of defects in property and supplants and abrogates all common law liability, rights, duties, obligations and remedies therefore.

§838. Applicability and Construction of Act

A.   This act does not apply to:
1.   Transfers pursuant to court order, including, but not limited to, transfers pursuant to a writ of execution, transfers by eminent domain and transfers pursuant to an order for partition;
2.   Transfers to a mortgagee by a mortgagor or successor in interest who is in default, transfers by any foreclosure sale after default in an obligation secured by a mortgage, transfers by a mortgagee's sale under a power of sale after default in an obligation secured by any instrument containing a power of sale, or transfers by a mortgagee who has acquired the real property at a sale conducted pursuant to a power of sale or a sale pursuant to a decree of foreclosure or has acquired the real property by deed in lieu of foreclosure;
3.   Transfers by a fiduciary who is not an owner occupant of the subject property in the course of the administration of a decedent's estate, guardianship, conservatorship or trust;
4.   Transfers from one co-owner to one or more other co-owners;
5.   Transfers made to a spouse, or to the person or persons in the lineal line of consanguinity of one or more of the owners;
6.   Transfers between spouses resulting from a decree of dissolution of marriage or a decree of legal separation or from a property settlement agreement incidental to such a decree;
7.   Transfers made pursuant to mergers and from a subsidiary to a parent or the reverse;
8.   Transfers or exchanges to or from any governmental entity; or
9.   Transfers of a newly constructed, previously unoccupied dwelling.

B.   Nothing in this act shall be construed to alter or change the requirements of Section 858-513 of Title 59 of the Oklahoma Statutes, regarding psychologically impacted real estate.

§838. Form of Notices or Acknowledgments

Any notices or acknowledgments required under this act need not be sworn to, verified or acknowledged.

Oklahoma Residential Landlord

and Tenant Act

41 O.S. §§, 51-52, 61

Title 41. Landlord and Tenant

§51. Definitions

As used in this act:
1. "Landlord" means the owner, lessor or sublessor of a nonresidential rental property, but does not mean an "owner" as defined by Section 192 of Title 42 of the Oklahoma Statutes;
2. "Nonresidential rental property" means any land or building which is rented or leased to a tenant for other than residential purposes and the rental agreement of which is not regulated under the provisions of the Oklahoma Residential Landlord and Tenant Act, Section 101 et seq. of Title 41 of the Oklahoma Statutes or the Self-Service Storace Facility Lien Act, Section 191 et seq. of Title 42 of the Oklahoma Statutes; and
3. "Tenant" means any person entitled under a rental agreement to occupy the nonresidential rental property.

§51. When Tenant Abandons, Surrenders Possession of, or is Evicted from Nonresidential Rental Property - Disposition of Personal Property of Tenant - Notice - Costs of Storage - Landlord Liability - Proceeds of Sale

A. If a tenant abandons, surrenders possession of, or is evicted from nonresidential rental property and leaves goods, furnishings, fixtures, or any other personal property on the premises of the nonresidential rental property, the landlord may take possession of the personal property ten (10) days after the tenant receives personal service of notice or fifteen (15) days after notice is mailed, whichever is latest, and if the personal property has no ascertainable or apparent value, the landlord may dispose of the personal property in a reasonable commercial manner. In any such case, the landlord has the option of complying with the provisions of subsection B of this section.

B. If the tenant abandons, surrenders possession of, or is evicted from the nonresidential rental property and leaves goods, furnishings, fixtures, or any other personal property of an ascertainable or apparent value on the premises of the nonresidential rental property, the landlord may take possession of the personal property and give notice to the tenant, demanding that the personal property be removed within the dates set out in the notice but not less than fifteen (15) days after delivery or mailing of such notice, and that if the personal property is not removed within the time specified in the notice, the landlord may sell the personal property at a public sale. The landlord may dispose of perishable commodities in any manner the landlord considers fit. Payment by the tenant of all outstanding rent, damages, storage fees, court costs and attorneys' fees shall be a prerequisite to the return of the personal property. For purposes of this section, notice sent by registered or certified mail to the tenant's last-known address with forwarding requested shall be deemed sufficient notice.

C. After notice is given as provided in subsection B of this section, the landlord shall store all personal property of the tenant in a place of safekeeping and shall exercise reasonable care of the personal property. The landlord shall not be responsible to the tenant for any loss not caused by the landlord's deliberate or negligent act. The landlord may elect to store the personal property on the premises of the nonresidential rental property that was abandoned or surrendered by the tenant or from which the tenant was evicted, in which event the storage cost may not exceed the fair rental value of the premises. If the tenant's personal property is removed to a commercial storage company, the storage cost shall include the actual charge for the storage and removal from the premises to the place of storage.

D. If the tenant makes timely response in writing of an intention to remove the personal property from the premises and does not do so within the later of the time specified in the notice provided for in subsection B of this section or within fifteen (15) days of the delivery or mailing of the tenant's written response, it shall be conclusively presumed that the tenant abandoned the personal property. If the tenant removes the personal property within the time limitations provided in this subsection, the landlord is entitled to the cost of storage for the period during which the personal property remained in the landlord's safekeeping plus all other costs that accrued under the rental agreement.

E. If the tenant fails to take possession of the personal property as prescribed in subsection D of this section and make payment of all amounts due and owing, the personal property shall be deemed abandoned and the landlord may thereupon sell the personal property in any reasonable manner without liability to the tenant.

F. Notice of sale shall be mailed to the owner and any other party claiming any interest in said personal property, if known, at their last-known post office address, by certified or registered mail at least ten (10) days before the time specified therein for such sale. For purposes of this section, parties who claim an interest in the personal property include holders of security interests or other liens or encumbrances as shown by the records in the office of the county clerk of the county where the lien would be foreclosed.

G. The landlord or any other person may in good faith become a purchaser of the personal property sold. The landlord may dispose of any personal property upon which no bid is made at the public sale.

H. The landlord may not be held to respond in damages in an action by a tenant claiming loss by reason of the landlord's election to destroy, sell or otherwise dispose of the personal property in compliance with the provisions of this section. If, however, the landlord deliberately or negligently violated the provisions of this section, the landlord shall be liable for actual damages.

I. Any proceeds from the sale or other disposition of the personal property, as provided in subsection B of this section, shall be applied by the landlord in the following order:

(1) To the reasonable expenses of taking, holding, preparing for sale or disposition, giving notice and selling or disposing thereof;

(2) To the satisfaction of any properly recorded security interest;

(3) To the satisfaction of any amount due from the tenant to the landlord for rent or otherwise; and

(4) The balance, if any, shall be paid into court within thirty (30) days of the sale and held for six (6) months and, if not claimed by the owner of the personal property within that period, shall escheat to the county.

§61. Method for Computation of Time

The time within which an act is to be done, as provided for in Title 41 of the Oklahoma Statutes, shall be computed by excluding the first day and including the last day. If the last day is a legal holiday as defined by Section 82.1 of Title 25 of the Oklahoma Statutes, it shall be excluded. The provisions of this section are hereby declared to be a clarification of the law as it existed prior to the effective date of this act and shall not be considered or construed to be a change of the law as it existed prior to the effective date of this act. Any action or proceeding arising under Title 41 of the Oklahoma Statutes prior to the effective date of this act for which a determination of the period of time prescribed by this section is in question or has been in question due to the enactment of Section 20, Chapter 293, O.S.L. 1999, shall be governed by the method for computation of time as prescribed by this section.

41 O.S. §§101-136 - Residential Landlord and Tenant Act

§101. Short Title

This act shall be known and may be cited as the **"Oklahoma Residential Landlord and Tenant Act."**

§102. Definitions

Unless the context otherwise requires:

1. "Building and housing codes" means any law, ordinance or governmental regulation concerning fitness for habitation or the construction, maintenance, operation, occupancy, use or appearance of any premises or dwelling unit;

2. "Deposit" means any money or other property required by a landlord from a tenant as a security and which is to be returned to the tenant upon termination of the rental agreement, less any deductions properly made and allowed by this act;

3. "Dwelling unit" means a structure, or that part of a structure, which is used as a home, residence or sleeping place by one or more persons, and includes any site, space or lot leased to the owner or resident of a manufactured or mobile home;

4. "Good faith" means honesty in fact in the conduct of the transaction concerned;

5. "Landlord" means the owner, lessor or sublessor of the dwelling unit or the building of which it is a part, manufactured or mobile home site, space or lot, and it also means a manager of the premises who fails to comply with the disclosure provisions of Section 116 of this title;

6. "Occupant" means any person who abides within a dwelling unit, or any person who owns or occupies a manufactured or mobile home, but who is not a tenant or an unemancipated minor child of a tenant, and who is not legally obligated by the terms of a rental agreement;

7. "Organization" means a corporation, government, governmental subdivision or agency, business trust, estate, trust, partnership or association, two or more persons having a joint or common interest and any other legal or commercial entity;

8. "Owner" means one or more persons, jointly or severally, in whom is vested:
   a   all or any part of the legal title to the property, or
   b   all or part of the beneficial ownership and a right to present use and enjoyment of the property, and such term includes a mortgagee in possession;

9. "Person" means an individual or organization;

10. "Premises" means a dwelling unit and the structure of which it is a part, the facilities and appurtenances therein, the site, space or lot leased to the owner or resident of a mobile or manufactured home, and the grounds, areas and facilities held out for the use of the tenant generally or the use of which is promised to the tenant;

11. "Rent" means all payments, except deposits and damages, to be made to the landlord under the rental agreement;

12. "Rental agreement" means all agreements and valid rules and regulations adopted under Section 126 of this title, which establish, embody or modify the terms and conditions concerning the use and occupancy of a dwelling unit and premises;

13. "Roomer" or "boarder" means a tenant occupying a dwelling unit:
   a   which lacks at least one major bathroom or kitchen facility, such as a toilet, refrigerator or stove,
   b   in a building
      (1)   where one or more of such major facilities are supplied to be used in common by the occupants of the roomer or boarder's dwelling unit and one or more other dwelling units, and
      (2)   in which the landlord resides;

14. "Single-family residence" means a structure used and maintained as a single dwelling unit. A dwelling unit, including those with common walls, shall be deemed a single-family residence if it has direct access to a street or thoroughfare and shares neither heating facilities, hot water equipment, nor any other essential facility or service with any other dwelling unit; and

15. "Tenant" means any person entitled under a rental agreement to occupy a dwelling unit.

§103. Application of Act

A. Except as otherwise provided in this act, this act applies to, regulates and determines rights, obligations and remedies under a rental agreement, wherever made, for a dwelling unit located within this state.

B. Any agreement, whether written or oral, shall be unenforceable insofar as said agreement, or any provision thereof, conflicts with any provision of this act.

§104. Arrangements not covered by act

Unless created to avoid the application of this act, the following arrangements are not governed by this act:

1. Residence at an institution, public or private, if incidental to detention or the provision of medical, geriatric, educational, counseling, religious or similar service;

2. Occupancy under a contract of sale or contract for deed of a dwelling unit or of the property of which it is a part, if the occupant is the purchaser or a person who succeeds to his interest;
3. Occupancy by a member of a fraternal or social organization in a structure operated for the benefit of the organization;
4. Transient occupancy in a hotel, motel or other similar lodging;
5. Occupancy by an owner of a condominium unit or a holder of a proprietary lease in a cooperative; and
6. Occupancy under a rental agreement covering premises used by the occupant primarily for agricultural purposes.

§105. Mitigation of damages—Rights, obligations and remedies—Enforcement

A. An aggrieved party under the provisions of this act has a duty to mitigate damages.
B. Any right, obligation or remedy declared by this act is enforceable in any court of appropriate jurisdiction including small claims court and may be prosecuted as part of an action for forcible entry or detainer unless the provision declaring it specifies a different and limited effect. In any action for breach of a rental agreement or to enforce any right or obligation provided for in this act, the prevailing party shall be entitled to reasonable attorneys' fees.

§106. Settlement of claim

A claim or right arising under this act or a rental agreement, if disrupted in good faith, may be settled by agreement and requires no further consideration.

§107. Good faith performance or enforcement

Every duty under this act and every act which must be performed as a condition precedent to the exercise of a right or remedy under this act imposes an obligation of good faith in its performance or enforcement.

§108. Beneficial owner to maintain premises

Any agreement, assignment, conveyance, trust deed or security instrument which authorizes a person other than the beneficial owner to act as landlord of a dwelling unit shall not relieve the beneficial owner of the duty to conform with this act and any other law, code, ordinance or regulation concerning the maintenance and operation of the premises.

§109. Rent

A. In the absence of agreement, the occupants of a dwelling unit shall pay to the landlord as rent the fair rental value for the use and occupancy of the dwelling unit.
B. Rent shall be payable at the time and place agreed to by the parties. Unless otherwise agreed, the entire rent shall be payable at the dwelling unit at the beginning of any term of one (1) month or less, while one (1) month's rent shall be payable at the beginning of each month of a longer term.

§110. Term of tenancy

Unless the rental agreement fixes a definite term in writing, the tenancy is week-to-week in the case of a roomer or boarder who pays weekly rent, and in all other cases month-to-month.

§111. Termination of tenancy

A. Except as otherwise provided in the Oklahoma Residential Landlord and Tenant Act, when the tenancy is month-to-month or tenancy at will, the landlord or tenant may terminate the tenancy provided the landlord or tenant gives a written notice to the other at least thirty (30) days before the date upon which the termination is to become effective. The thirty day period to terminate shall begin to run from the date notice to terminate is served as provided in subsection E of this section.
B. Except as otherwise provided in the Oklahoma Residential Landlord and Tenant Act, when the tenancy is less than month-to-month, the landlord or tenant may terminate the tenancy provided the landlord or tenant gives to the

other a written notice served as provided in subsection E of this section at least seven (7) days before the date upon which the termination is to become effective.

C. Unless earlier terminated under the provisions of the Oklahoma Residential Landlord and Tenant Act or unless otherwise agreed upon, a tenancy for a definite term expires on the ending date thereof without notice.

D. If the tenant remains in possession without the landlord's consent after the expiration of the term of the rental agreement or its termination under the Oklahoma Residential Landlord and Tenant Act, the landlord may immediately bring an action for possession and damages. If the tenant's holdover is willful and not in good faith the landlord may also recover an amount not more than twice the average monthly rental, computed and prorated on a daily basis, for each month or portion thereof that said tenant remains in possession. If the landlord consents to the tenant's continued occupancy, a month-to-month tenancy is thus created, unless the parties otherwise agree.

E. The written notice, required by the Oklahoma Residential Landlord and Tenant Act, to terminate any tenancy shall be served on the tenant or landlord personally unless otherwise specified by law. If the tenant cannot be located, service shall be made by delivering the notice to any family member of such tenant over the age of twelve (12) years residing with tenant. If service cannot be made on the tenant personally or on such family member, notice shall be posted at a conspicuous place on the dwelling unit of the tenant. If the notice is posted, a copy of such notice shall be mailed to the tenant by certified mail. If service cannot be made on the landlord personally, the notice shall be mailed to the landlord by certified mail. For the purpose of this subsection, the word "landlord" shall mean any person authorized to receive service of process and notice pursuant to Section 116 of this title.

§112. Duties of Parties upon Termination of Tenancy

Except as otherwise provided in this act, whenever either party to a rental agreement rightfully elects to terminate, the duties of each party under the rental agreement shall cease and be determined upon the effective date of said termination, and the parties shall thereupon discharge any remaining obligations under this act as soon as practicable.

§113. Rental Agreements

A. A rental agreement may not provide that either party thereto:
  1. Agrees to waive or forego rights or remedies under this act;
  2. Authorizes any person to confess judgment on a claim arising out of the rental agreement;
  3. Agrees to pay the other party's attorney's fees;
  4. Agrees to the exculpation, limitation or indemnification of any liability arising under law for damages or injuries to persons or property caused by or resulting from the acts or omissions of either party, their agents, servants or employees in the operation or maintenance of the dwelling unit or the premises of which it is a part; or
  5. Agrees to the establishment of a lien except as allowed by this act in and to the property of the other party.

B. A provision prohibited by subsection A of this section and included in a rental agreement is unenforceable.

§113a. Flooding within Past 5 Years to be Disclosed in Written Rental Agreements – Failure to Disclose

A. If the premises to be rented has been flooded within the past five (5) years and such fact is known to the landlord, the landlord shall include such information prominently and in writing as part of any written rental agreements. Failure to provide such information shall entitle any tenant who is a party to the rental agreement to sue the landlord of the premises in a court of appropriate jurisdiction and to recover the personal property damages sustained by the tenant from flooding of the premises.

B. For the purpose of this section, "flooded and flooding" shall mean general and temporary conditions of partial or complete inundation of normally dry land areas and structures upon said areas from the overflow of lakes, ponds, streams, rivers, creeks and any other inland waters.

§113.1. Denial or Termination of Tenancy to Blind Person Because of Guide Dog

A landlord shall not deny or terminate a tenancy to a blind, deaf, or physically handicapped person because of the guide, signal, or service dog of such person unless such dogs are specifically prohibited in the rental agreement entered into prior to Nov. 1,1985.

§114. Alienees—Rights, Obligations and Remedies

Alienees of landlords and tenants shall have the same legal rights, obligations and remedies as their principals.

§115. Damage or Security Deposits

A. Any damage or security deposit required by a landlord of a tenant must be kept in an escrow account for the tenant, which account shall be maintained in the State of Oklahoma with a federally insured financial institution. Misappropriation of the security deposit shall be unlawful and punishable by a term in a county jail not to exceed six (6) months and by a fine in an amount not to exceed twice the amount misappropriated from the escrow account.

B. Upon termination of the tenancy, any security deposit held by the landlord may be applied to the payment of accrued rent and the amount of damages which the landlord has suffered by reason of the tenant's noncompliance with this act and the rental agreement, all as itemized by the landlord in a written statement delivered by mail to be by return receipt requested and to be signed for by any person of statutory service age at such address or in person to the tenant if he can reasonably be found. If the landlord proposes to retain any portion of the security deposit for rent, damages or other legally allowable charges under the provisions of this act or the rental agreement, the landlord shall return the balance of the security deposit without interest to the tenant within thirty (30) days after the termination of tenancy, delivery of possession and written demand by the tenant. If the tenant does not make such written demand of such deposit within six (6) months after termination of the tenancy, the deposit reverts to the landlord in consideration of the costs and burden of maintaining the escrow account, and the interest of the tenant in that deposit terminates at that time.

C. Upon cessation of a landlord's interest in the dwelling unit including, but not limited to, termination of interest by sale, assignment, death, bankruptcy, appointment of receiver or otherwise, the person in possession of the tenant's damage or security deposits at his option or pursuant to court order shall, within a reasonable time:
    1. Transfer said deposits to the landlord's successor in interest and notify the tenants in writing of such transfer and of the transferee's name and address; or
    2. Return the deposits to the tenants.

D. Upon receipt of the transferred deposits under paragraph 1 of subsection C of this section, the transferee, in relation to such deposits, shall have all the rights and obligations of a landlord holding such deposits under this act.

E. If a landlord or manager fails to comply with this section or fails to return any prepaid rent required to be paid to a tenant under this act, the tenant may recover the damage and security deposit and prepaid rent, if any.

F. Except as otherwise provided by the rental agreement, a tenant shall not apply or deduct any portion of the security deposit from the last month's rent or use or apply such tenant's security deposit at any time in lieu of payment of rent.

G. This section does not preclude the landlord or tenant from recovering other damages to which he may be entitled under this act.

§116. Person to Accept Service or Notice— Identity of Owner and Manager—Failure to Comply with Section

A. As a part of any rental agreement the lessor shall prominently and in writing identify what person at what address is entitled to accept service or notice under this act. The landlord or any person authorized to enter into a rental agreement on his behalf shall disclose to the tenant in writing at or before the commencement of the tenancy the name and address of:
    1. The person or persons authorized to manage the premises;
    2. The owner or owners of the premises; or
    3. The name and address of a person authorized to act for and on behalf of the owner for the purpose of receipt of service of process and receiving and receipting for notices.
        The information required to be furnished by this section shall be kept current and this section extends to and is enforceable against any successor owner, landlord or manager.

B. A person who fails to comply with this section becomes a landlord for the purposes of this act and an agent of each person who is otherwise a landlord for:
    1. Receipt of service of process and receiving and receipting for notices and demands; and
    2. Performing the obligations of a landlord under this act and under the rental agreement and expending and making available for the purpose all rents collected from the premises.

Oklahoma Residential Landlord and Tenant Act

§117. Commencement of Tenancy—Delivery of Possession—Wrongful Possession

    A. At the commencement of the term a landlord shall deliver full possession of the premises to the tenant in compliance with the rental agreement and Section 118 of this title. Except as otherwise provided in this act, the landlord may bring an action for possession against any other person wrongfully in possession and may recover his damages.

    B. A rental agreement may provide reasonable limitations upon use of a dwelling unit or premises by a tenant or occupant. A landlord shall have the right to demand that an occupant vacate the dwelling unit or the premises or both if such occupant breaches any condition of the rental agreement which would be enforceable against the tenant. If a landlord makes a written request to the tenant or to the occupant for the occupant to depart from the dwelling unit or the premises or both, the occupant shall comply. If the occupant wrongfully fails to comply within a reasonable time, the occupant shall, upon conviction, be deemed guilty of a trespass and may be punished by a fine of not to exceed Five Hundred Dollars ($500.00) or by confinement in the county jail for a period not to exceed thirty (30) days or by both such fine and imprisonment.

    C. An occupancy limitation of two (2) persons per bedroom residing in a dwelling unit shall be presumed reasonable for this state. The two-person limitation shall not apply to a child or children born to the tenants during the course of the lease.

§118. Duties of Landlord and Tenant

A. A landlord shall at all times during the tenancy:
1. Except in the case of a single-family residence, keep all common areas of his building, grounds, facilities and appurtenances in a clean, safe and sanitary condition;
2. Makeallrepairsanddowhateverisnecessarytoputandkeepthetenant'sdwellingunitand premises in a fit and habitable condition;
3. Maintain in good and safe working order and condition all electrical, plumbing, sanitary, heating, ventilating, air-conditioning and other facilities and appliances, including elevators, sup- plied or required to be supplied by him;
4. Except in the case of one-or two-family residences or where provided by a governmental entity, provide and maintain appropriate receptacles and conveniences for the removal of ashes, garbage, rubbish and other waste incidental to the occupancy of the dwelling unit and arrange for the frequent removal of such wastes; and
5. Except in the case of a single-family residence or where the service is supplied by direct and independently-metered utility connections to the dwelling unit, supply running water and reasonable amounts of hot water at all times and reasonable heat.

B. The landlord and tenant of a dwelling unit may agree by a conspicuous writing independent of the rental agreement that the tenant is to perform specified repairs, maintenance tasks, alterations or remodeling.

C. Prior to the commencement of a rental agreement, if a landlord knows or has reason to know that the dwelling unit or any part of the premises was used in the manufacture of methamphetamine, the landlord shall disclose this information to a prospective tenant. Provided however, if the landlord has had the level of contamination assessed within the dwelling unit or pertinent part of the premises, and it has been determined that the level of contamination does not exceed one-tenth of one microgram (0.1 mcg) per one hundred square centimemeters (100 cm2) of surface materials within the dwelling unit or pertinent part of the premises, no disclosure shall be required.

§119. Conveyance of Property—Attornment of Tenant

    A. A conveyance of real estate or of any interest therein, by a landlord shall be valid without the attornment of the tenant, but the payment of rent by the tenant to the grantor at any time before written notice of the conveyance is given to the tenant shall be good against the grantee.

    B. The attornment of a tenant to a stranger shall be void, and shall not affect the possession of the landlord unless it is made with the consent of the landlord, or pursuant to a judgment at law, or the order or decree of a court.

    C. Unless otherwise agreed and except as otherwise provided in this act, upon termination of the owner's interest in the dwelling unit including, but not limited to, termination of interest by sale, assignment, death, bankruptcy, appointment of a receiver or otherwise, the owner is relieved of all liability under the rental agreement and of all obligations under this act as to events occurring subsequent to written notice to the resident of the termination of the owner's interest. The successor in interest to the owner shall be liable for all obligations under the rental agreement or under this act. Upon receipt by a resident of written notice of the termination of the owner's interest in the dwelling unit, a resident shall pay all future rental payments, when due, to the successor in interest to the owner.

D. Unless otherwise agreed and except as otherwise provided in this act, a manager of premises that includes a dwelling unit is relieved of liability under a rental agreement and this act as to events occurring after written notice to the tenant of the termination of his management.

§120. Failure of Landlord to Deliver Possession of Dwelling Unit to Tenant

A. If the landlord fails to deliver possession of the dwelling unit to the tenant, rent abates until possession is delivered and the tenant may terminate the rental agreement by giving a written notice of such termination to the landlord, whereupon the landlord shall return all prepaid rent and deposit, or the tenant may, at his option, demand performance of the rental agreement by the landlord and maintain an action for possession of the dwelling unit against any person wrongfully in possession and recover the actual damages sustained by him.

B. If a person's failure to deliver possession is willful and not in good faith, an aggrieved person may recover from that person an amount not more than twice the monthly rental as specified in the rental agreement, computed and prorated on a daily basis, for each month, or portion thereof, that said person wrongfully remains in possession.

§121. Landlord's Breach of Rental Agreement—Deductions from Rent for Repairs—Failure to Supply Heat, Water or Other Essential Services—Habitability of Dwelling Unit

A. Except as otherwise provided in this act, if there is a material noncompliance by the landlord with the terms of the rental agreement or a noncompliance with any of the provisions of Section 18 of this act which noncompliance materially affects health or safety, the tenant may deliver to the landlord a written notice specifying the acts and omissions constituting the breach and that the rental agreement will terminate upon a date not less than thirty (30) days after receipt of the notice if the breach is not remedied within fourteen (14) days, and thereafter the rental agreement shall so terminate as provided in the notice unless the landlord adequately remedies the breach within the time specified.

B. Except as otherwise provided in this act, if there is a material noncompliance by the landlord with any of the terms of the rental agreement or any of the provisions of Section 18 of this act which noncompliance materially affects health and the breach is remediable by repairs, the reasonable cost of which is less than One Hundred Dollars ($100.00), the tenant may notify the landlord in writing of his intention to correct the condition at the landlord's expense after the expiration of fourteen (14) days. If the landlord fails to comply within said fourteen (14) days, or as promptly as conditions require in the case of an emergency, the tenant may thereafter cause the work to be done in a workmanlike manner and, after submitting to the landlord an itemized statement, deduct from his rent the actual and reasonable cost or the fair and reasonable value of the work, not exceeding the amount specified in this subsection, in which event the rental agreement shall not terminate by reason of that breach.

C. Except as otherwise provided in this act, if, contrary to the rental agreement or Section 18 of this act, the landlord willfully or negligently fails to supply heat, running water, hot water, electric, gas or other essential service, the tenant may give written notice to the landlord specifying the breach and thereafter may:

1. Upon written notice, immediately terminate the rental agreement; or
2. Procure reasonable amounts of heat, hot water, running water, electric, gas or other essential service during the period of the landlord's noncompliance and deduct their actual and reasonable cost from the rent; or
3. Recover damages based upon the diminution of the fair rental value of the dwelling unit; or
4. Upon written notice, procure reasonable substitute housing during the period of the landlord's noncompliance, in which case the tenant is excused from paying rent for the period of the landlord's noncompliance.

D. Except as otherwise provided in this act, if there is a noncompliance by the landlord with the terms of the rental agreement or Section 18 of this act, which noncompliance renders the dwelling unit uninhabitable or poses an imminent threat to the health and safety of any occupant of the dwelling unit and which noncompliance is not remedied as promptly as conditions require, the tenant may immediately terminate the rental agreement upon written notice to the landlord which notice specifies the noncompliance.

E. All rights of the tenant under this section do not arise until he has given written notice to the landlord or if the condition complained of was caused by the deliberate or negligent act or omission of the tenant, a member of his family, his animal or pet or other person or animal on the premises with his consent.

§122. Damage to or Destruction of Dwelling Unit—Rights and Duties of Tenant

A. If the dwelling unit or premises are damaged or destroyed by fire or other casualty to an extent that enjoyment of the dwelling unit is substantially impaired, unless the impairment is caused by the deliberate or negligent act or omission of the tenant, a member of his family, his animal or pet or other person or animal on the premises with his consent, the tenant may:
   1. Immediately vacate the premises and notify the landlord in writing within one (1) week thereafter of his intention to terminate the rental agreement, in which case the rental agreement terminates as of the date of vacating; or
   2. If continued occupancy is possible, vacate any part of the dwelling unit rendered unusable by the fire or casualty, in which case the tenant's liability for rent is reduced in proportion to the diminution in the fair rental value of the dwelling unit.
B. If the rental agreement is terminated under this section the landlord shall return all deposits recoverable under Section 115 of this act and all prepaid and unearned rent. Accounting for rent in the event of termination or apportionment shall be made as of the date of the fire or other casualty.

§123. Wrongful Removal or Exclusion from Dwelling Unit

If a landlord wrongfully removes or excludes a tenant from possession of a dwelling unit, the tenant may recover possession by a proceeding brought in a court of competent jurisdiction, or terminate the rental agreement after giving notice of such intention to the landlord, and in either case recover an amount not more than twice the average monthly rental, or twice his actual damages, whichever is greater. If the rental agreement is terminated, the landlord shall return all deposits recoverable under Section 115 of this act and all prepaid and unearned rent.

§124. Unlawful Entry or Lawful Entry in Unreasonable Manner—Harassment of Tenant— Damages

A. If the landlord makes an unlawful entry or a lawful entry in an unreasonable manner or harasses the tenant by making repeated unreasonable demands for entry, the tenant may obtain injunctive relief to prevent the recurrence of the conduct or, upon written notice, terminate the rental agreement. In either case the tenant may recover actual damages.
B. Neither injunctive relief nor damages shall be available to a tenant if the basis for the land- lord's action is the landlord's execution of a writ in the manner prescribed by Section 1148. 10A of Title 12 of the Oklahoma Statutes.

§125. Defective Condition of Premises— Report to Landlord

Any defective condition of the premises which comes to the tenant's attention, and which the tenant has reason to believe is unknown to the landlord, shall be reported by the tenant to the landlord as soon as practicable.

§126. Tenant's Use and Occupancy of Premises—Rules and Regulations

A. A landlord, from time to time, may adopt a rule or regulation, however described, concerning the tenant's use and occupancy of the premises. Such a rule or regulation is enforceable against the tenant only if:
   1. Its purpose is to promote the convenience, peace, safety or welfare of the tenants in the premises, preserve the landlord's property from abusive use, or make a fair distribution of services and facilities held out for the tenants generally; and
   2. It is reasonably related to the purpose for which it is adopted; and
   3. It applies to all tenants in the premises in a fair manner; and
   4. It is sufficiently explicit in its prohibition, direction or limitation of the tenant's conduct to fairly inform the tenant what such tenant must or must not do to comply; and
   5. It is not for the purpose of evading the obligations of the landlord; and

6. The tenant has notice of it at the time such tenant enters into the rental agreement, or when it is adopted.

B. If a rule or regulation is adopted after the tenant enters into the rental agreement and that rule or regulation works a substantial modification of such tenant's bargain, the rule or regulation so adopted is not valid and enforceable against the tenant unless he consents to it in writing.

§127. Duties of Tenant

The tenant shall at all times during the tenancy:

1. Keep that part of the premises which such tenant occupies and uses as safe, clean and sanitary as the condition of the premises permits;
2. Dispose from such tenant's dwelling unit all ashes, garbage, rubbish and other waste in a safe, clean and sanitary manner;
3. Keep all plumbing fixtures in the dwelling unit or used by the tenant as clean and sanitary as their condition permits;
4. Use in a safe and nondestructive manner all electrical, plumbing, sanitary, heating, ventilating, air-conditioning and other facilities and appliances including elevators in the premises;
5. Not deliberately or negligently destroy, deface, damage, impair or remove any part of the premises or permit any person, animal or pet to do so;
6. Not engage in conduct or allow any person or animal or pet, on the premises with the express or implied permission or consent of the tenant, to engage in conduct that will disturb the quiet and peaceful enjoyment of the premises by other tenants;
7. Comply with all covenants, rules, regulations and the like which are in accordance with Section 126 of this title; and
8. Not engage in criminal activity that threatens the health, safety right of peaceful enjoyment of the premises by other tenants or is a danger to the premises, and not engage in any drug-related criminal activity on or near the premises either personally or by any member of the tenant's household or any guest or other person under the tenant's control.

§128. Consent of Tenant for Landlord to Enter Dwelling Unit—Emergency Entry —Abuse of Right of Entry — Notice—Abandoned Premises—Refusal of Consent

A. A tenant shall not unreasonably withhold consent to the landlord, his agents and employees, to enter into the dwelling unit in order to inspect the premises, make necessary or agreed repairs, decorations, alterations or improvements, supply necessary or agreed services or exhibit the dwelling unit to prospective or actual purchasers, mortgagee, tenants, workmen or contractors.
B. A landlord, his agents and employees may enter the dwelling unit without consent of the tenant in case of emergency.
C. A landlord shall not abuse the right of access or use it to harass the tenant. Except in case of emergency or unless it is impracticable to do so, the landlord shall give the tenant at least one (1) day's notice of his intent to enter and may enter only at reasonable times.
D. Unless the tenant has abandoned or surrendered the premises, a landlord has no other right of access during a tenancy except as is provided in this act or pursuant to a court order.
E. If the tenant refuses to allow lawful access, the landlord may obtain injunctive relief to compel access or he may terminate the rental agreement.

§129. Tenant's Breach of Rental Agreement—Wrongful Abandonment

A. Unless otherwise agreed, use by the tenant of the dwelling unit for any purpose other than as his place of abode shall constitute a breach of the rental agreement and shall be grounds of terminating the rental agreement.
B. If the tenant wrongfully quits and abandons the dwelling unit during the term of the tenancy, the landlord shall make reasonable efforts to make the dwelling unit available for rental. If the landlord rents the dwelling unit for a term beginning before the expiration of the rental agreement, said rental agreement terminates as of the commencement date of the new tenancy. If the landlord fails to use reasonable efforts to make the dwelling unit available for rental or if the landlord accepts the abandonment as surrender, the rental agreement is

deemed to be terminated by the landlord as of the date the landlord has notice of the abandonment. If, after making reasonable efforts to make the dwelling unit available for rental after the abandonment, the landlord fails to re-rent the premises for a fair rental during the term, the tenant shall be liable for the entire rent or the difference in rental, whichever may be appropriate, for the remainder of the term. If the tenancy is from month-to- month or week-to-week, the term of the rental agreement for this purpose is deemed to be a month or a week, as the case may be.

§130. Abandoning or Surrendering Possession of Dwelling Unit—Disposition of Personal Property

A. If the tenant abandons or surrenders possession of the dwelling unit or has been lawfully removed from the premises through eviction proceedings and leaves household goods, furnishings, fixtures, or any other personal property in the dwelling unit, the landlord may take possession of the property, and if, in the judgment of the landlord, the property has no ascertainable or apparent value, the landlord may dispose of the property without any duty of accounting or any liability to any party. The landlord may dispose of perishable property in any manner the landlord considers fit.

B. If the tenant abandons or surrenders possession of the dwelling unit or has been lawfully removed from the premises through eviction proceedings and leaves household goods, furnishings, fixtures, or any other personal property in the dwelling unit, the landlord may take possession of the property, and if, in the judgment of the landlord the property has an ascertainable or apparent value, the landlord shall provide written notice to the tenant by certified mail to the last-known address that if the property is not removed within the time specified in the notice, the property will be deemed abandoned. Any property left with the landlord for a period of thirty (30) days or longer shall be conclusively determined to be abandoned and as such the landlord may dispose of said property in any manner which he deems reasonable and proper without liability to the tenant or any other interested party.

C. The landlord shall store all personal property of the tenant in a place of safekeeping and shall exercise reasonable care of the property. The landlord shall not be responsible to the tenant for any loss not caused by the landlord's deliberate or negligent act. The landlord may elect to store the property in the dwelling unit that was abandoned or surrendered by the tenant, in which event the storage cost may not exceed the fair rental value of the premises. If the tenant's property is removed to a commercial storage company, the storage cost shall include the actual charge for the storage and removal from the premises to the place of storage.

D. If the tenant removes the personal property within the time limitation provided in this section, the landlord is entitled to the cost of storage for the period during which the property remained in the landlord's safekeeping plus all other costs that accrued under the rental agreement.

E. The landlord may not be held to respond in damages in an action by a tenant claiming loss by reason of the landlord's election to destroy, sell or otherwise dispose of the property in compliance with the provisions of this section. If, however, the landlord deliberately or negligently violated the provisions of this section, the landlord shall be liable for actual damages.

§130.1. Death of Tenant - Disposition of Personal Property

A. Upon written request of a landlord, the landlord's tenant shall:
   1. Provide the landlord with the name, address, and telephone number of a person to contact in the event of the tenant's death; and
   2. Sign a statement authorizing the landlord in the event of the tenant's death to:
      a. grant to the person designated under paragraph 1 of this subsection access to the premises at a reasonable time and in the presence of the landlord or the landlord's agent,
      b. allow the person designated under paragraph 1 of this subsection to remove any of the tenant's property found at the leased premises, and
      c. refund the tenant's security deposit, less lawful deductions, to the person designated under paragraph 1 of this subsection.

B. A tenant may, without request from the landlord, provide the landlord with the information specified in subsection A of this section.

C. Except as provided in subsection D of this section, in the event of the death of a tenant who is the sole occupant of a rental dwelling:
   1. The landlord may remove and store all property found in the tenant's leased premises;

2. The landlord shall turn over possession of the property to the person who was designated by the tenant under subsection A or B of this section or to any other person lawfully entitled to the property if the request is made prior to the property being discarded pursuant to paragraph 5 of this subsection;
3. The landlord shall refund the tenant's security deposit, less lawful deductions, including the cost of removing and storing the property, to the person designated under subsection A or B of this section or to any other person lawfully entitled to the refund;
4. Any person who removes property from the tenant's leased premises shall sign an inventory of the property being removed at the time of removal and submit the signed inventory to the landlord; and
5. The landlord may discard the property removed by the landlord from the tenant's leased premises if:
    a. the landlord has mailed a written request by certified mail, return receipt requested, to the person designated under subsection A or B of this section, requesting that the property be removed,
    b. the person failed to remove the property by the thirtieth day after the postmark date of the notice, and
    c. the landlord, prior to the date of discarding the property, has not been contacted by anyone claiming the property.

D. In a written lease or other agreement, a landlord and a tenant may agree to a procedure different than the procedure in this section for removing, storing, or disposing of property in the leased premises of a deceased tenant
E. If a tenant, after being furnished with a notice of request, knowingly violates subsection A of this section by failing to provide the required information and statement, the landlord shall have no responsibility after the tenant's death for removal, storage, disappearance, damage, or disposition of property in the tenant's leased premises.
F. If a landlord, after being furnished with a copy of this section, knowingly violates subsection C of this section, the landlord shall be liable to the estate of the deceased tenant for actual damages.

§131. Delinquent Rent

A. If rent is unpaid when due, the landlord may bring an action for recovery of the rent at any time thereafter or the landlord may wait until the expiration of the period allowed for curing a default by the tenant, as prescribed in subsection B of this section, before bringing such action.
B. A landlord may terminate a rental agreement for failure to pay rent when due, if the tenant fails to pay rent within five (5) days after written notice of landlord's demand for payment. The notice may be given before or after the landlord files any action authorized by subsection A of this section.

Demand for past due rent is deemed a demand for possession of the premises and no further notice to quit possession need be given by the landlord to the tenant for any purpose.

§132. Tenant's Failure to Comply with Rental Agreement or Perform Duties — Rights and Duties of Landlord

A. Except as otherwise provided in the Oklahoma Residential Landlord and Tenant Act, if there is a noncompliance by the tenant with the rental agreement or with Section 127 of this title which noncompliance can be remedied by repair, replacement of a damaged item, or cleaning and the tenant fails to comply as promptly as conditions require in the case of an emergency or within ten (10) days after written notice served as provided in subsection E of Section 111 of this title by the landlord specifying the breach and requiring that the tenant remedy it within that period of time, the landlord may enter the dwelling unit and cause the work to be done in a workmanlike manner and thereafter submit the itemized bill for the actual and reasonable cost or the fair and reasonable value thereof as rent on the next date rent is due, or if the rental agreement has terminated, for immediate payment. If the landlord remedies the breach as provided in this subsection, the landlord may not terminate the rental agreement by reason of the tenant's failure to remedy the breach.
B. Except as otherwise provided in the Oklahoma Residential Landlord and Tenant Act, if there is a material noncompliance by the tenant with the rental agreement or with any provision of Section 127 of this title, the landlord may deliver to the tenant a written notice served as provided in subsection E of Section 111 of this title specifying the acts and omissions constituting the noncompliance and that the rental agreement will terminate upon a date not less than fifteen (15) days after receipt of the notice unless remedied within ten (10) days. If the breach is not remedied within ten (10) days from receipt of the notice, the rental agreement shall terminate as provided in the notice. If within the ten (10) days the tenant adequately remedies the breach complained of, or if the landlord remedies the breach according to the provisions of subsection A of this

section, the rental agreement shall not terminate by reason of the breach. Any subsequent breach of the lease or noncompliance under this section shall be grounds, upon written notice to the tenant, for immediate termination of the lease.

C. Notwithstanding other provisions of this section, if there is a noncompliance by the tenant with the rental agreement or with any of the provisions of Section 127 of this title, which non- compliance causes or threatens to cause imminent and irremediable harm to the premises or to any person and which noncompliance is not remedied by the tenant as promptly as conditions require after the tenant has notice of it, the landlord may terminate the rental agreement by immediately filing a forcible entry and detainer action.

D. Any criminal activity that threatens the health, safety or right of peaceful enjoyment of the premises by other tenants committed by a tenant or by any member of the tenant's household or any guest or other person under the tenant's control or is a danger to the premises and any drug- related criminal activity on or near the premises by the tenant or by any member of the tenant's household or any guest or other person under the tenant's control shall be grounds for immediate termination of the lease.

§133. Lien on Tenant's property

A landlord shall have a lien upon that part of the property belonging to the tenant which has a reasonable relationship as nearly as practicable to the amount of the debt owed, which may be in a rental unit used by him at the time notice is given, for the proper charges owed by the tenant, and for the cost of enforcing the lien, with the right to possession of the property until the debt obligation is paid to the landlord. Provided, however, that such lien shall be secondary to the claim of any prior bona fide holder of a chattel mortgage or to the rights of a conditional seller of such property, other than the tenant.

For purposes of this section, property shall mean any baggage or other property belonging to the tenant which may be in the rental unit used by the tenant but which shall not include all tools, musical instruments or books used by the tenant in any trade or profession, all family portraits and pictures, all wearing apparel, any type of prosthetic or orthopedic appliance, hearing aid, glasses, false teeth, glass eyes, bedding, contraceptive devices, soap, tissues, washing machines, vaporizers, refrigerators, food, cooking and eating utensils, all other appliances personally used by the tenant for the protection of his health, or any baby bed or any other items used for the personal care of babies.

§134. Enforcement of Lien

A landlord lien may be enforced as any other general lien as provided in Section 91 of Title 42 of the Oklahoma Statutes.

§135. Construction of Act

This act shall be liberally construed and applied to promote and effectuate its underlying purposes and policies.

§136. Removal of Rented Furniture—Procedure

A. Upon termination of a furniture rental agreement, the lessor or agent of the lessor shall not remove the furniture from possession or dwelling place of the lessee unless the lessee or an agent of the lessee is present. Such furniture shall be marked with either an identifying number or in some other distinguishable manner prior to removal. Before the furniture is removed, the lessor or his agent shall inspect the furniture and advise the lessee or the agent of the lessee of each specific item of damage. If furniture is removed when such person is not present or if the furniture is not inspected before removal, the entire amount of any security deposit held by the lessor shall be returned to the lessee.

B. If the lessor complies with the provisions of subsection A of this Section and recovers dam- aged furniture, any security deposit held by the lessor may be applied to the amount of damages which the lessor has suffered due to the fault of the lessee if the lessor provides to the lessee a written itemized statement of damage delivered by mail, to be by return receipt requested and to be signed for by any person of statutory service age at such address. The lessor shall allow the lessee an opportunity to re-inspect the furniture in question before any security deposit may be retained or any additional damage charge made.

C. In the case of undamaged furniture, the lessor shall return any security deposit without interest to the lessee within thirty (30) days of the termination of the rental agreement. If the returned furniture is damaged, the lessor shall return the balance of any security deposit above the cost of damage, without interest, to the lessee within thirty (30) days of the inspection of the furniture by the lessee. If the lessee chooses not to inspect the furniture, the balance of the security deposit shall be returned to the lessee within thirty (30) days of the mailing of the written itemized statement of damage.

Oklahoma Fair Housing Law

Title 25, Article 4A, Section 1451 through Article 5 Section 1508

Article 4A. Discrimination in Housing

§25-1451. Definitions.

A. As used in Sections 1451 through 1453 of this title:
1. "Elderly person" means any natural person fifty-five (55) years of age or older;
2. "Dwelling" means:
a. any building, structure, or part of a building or structure that is occupied as, or designed or intended for occupancy as, a residence by one or more families, or
b. any vacant land that is offered for sale or lease for the construction or location of a building, structure, or part of a building or structure described in subparagraph a of this paragraph;
3. "Person" includes one or more individuals, corporations, partnerships, associations, labor organizations, legal representatives, mutual companies, joint-stock companies, trusts, unincorporated organizations, trustees, trustees in bankruptcy, receivers and fiduciaries, the state, and all political subdivisions and agencies thereof;
4. "Restrictive covenants" means any specification limiting the transfer, rental, or lease of any dwelling because of race, color, religion, sex, national origin, age, disability, or familial status;
5. "Discriminatory housing practices" means an act that is prohibited pursuant to Section 1452 of this title;
6. "Disability" means a mental or physical impairment that substantially limits at least one major life activity, when there is a record of such an impairment, or the individual is regarded as having such an impairment. The term does not include current illegal use of or addiction to any drug or illegal or federally controlled substance. For purposes of Sections 1451 through 1453 of this title, "an individual with a disability" or "disability" does not apply to an individual because of sexual orientation or the sexual preference of the individual or because that individual is a transvestite;
7. "Unlawful discriminatory practice because of age" means an act prohibited pursuant to Section 1452 of this title against a person at least eighteen (18) years of age or older solely on that basis;
8. "Aggrieved person" means any person who:
a. claims to have been injured by a discriminatory housing practice, or
b. believes that he or she will be injured by a discriminatory housing practice that is about to occur;
9. "Complainant" means a person or the Attorney General who files a complaint pursuant to Section 1452 of this title;
10. "Conciliation" means the attempted resolution of issues raised by a complaint or by the investigation of the complaint, through informal negotiations involving the aggrieved person, the respondent, and the Attorney General's Office of Civil Rights Enforcement;
11. "Conciliation agreement" means a written agreement setting forth the resolution of the issues in conciliation;
12. "Discriminatory housing practice" means an act prohibited by Section 1452 of this title;
13. "Family" includes a single individual;
14. "Respondent" means:
a. the person accused of a violation of Sections 1451 through 1453 of this title in a complaint of a discriminatory housing practice, or
b. any person identified as an additional or substitute respondent pursuant to Section 1502.5 of this title or an agent of an additional or substitute respondent; and
15. "To rent" means to lease, to sublease, to let, or to otherwise grant for a consideration the right to occupy premises not owned by the occupant.
B. For purposes of Sections 1451 through 1453 of this title, a discriminatory act is committed because of familial status only if the act is committed because the person who is the subject of discrimination is:
1. Pregnant;
2. Domiciled with an individual less than eighteen (18) years of age in regard to whom the person:
a. is the parent or legal custodian, or

b. has the written permission of the parent or legal custodian for domicile with that person; or

3. In the process of obtaining legal custody of an individual less than eighteen (18) years of age.

§25-1452. Unlawful Discriminatory Housing Practices

A. It shall be an unlawful discriminatory housing practice for any person, or any agent or employee of such person:

1. To refuse to sell or rent after the making of a bona fide offer, or to refuse to negotiate for the sale or rental of any housing, or otherwise make unavailable or deny any housing because of race, color, religion, gender, national origin, age, familial status, or disability;

2. To discriminate against any person in the terms, conditions, or privileges of sale or rental of housing, or in the provision of services or facilities in connection with any housing because of race, color, religion, gender, national origin, age, familial status, or disability;

3. To make, print, publish, or cause to be made, printed, or published any notice, statement, or advertisement, with respect to the sale or rental of housing that indicates any preference, limitation, discrimination, or intention to make any such preference, limitation, or discrimination because of race, color, religion, gender, national origin, age, familial status, or disability;

4. To represent to any person, for reasons of discrimination, that any housing is not available for inspection, sale, or rental when such housing is in fact so available because of race, color, religion, gender, national origin, age, familial status, or disability;

5. To deny any person access to, or membership or participation in, a multiple-listing service, real estate brokers' organization or other service, organization, or facility relating to the business of selling or renting dwellings, or discriminate against a person in the terms or conditions of access, membership, or participation in such an organization, service, or facility because of race, color, religion, gender, national origin, age, familial status, or disability;

6. To include in any transfer, sale, rental, or lease of housing any restrictive covenant that discriminates, or for any person to honor or exercise, or attempt to honor or exercise, any discriminatory covenant pertaining to housing because of race, color, religion, gender, national origin, age, familial status, or disability;

7. To refuse to consider the income of both applicants when both applicants seek to buy or lease housing because of race, color, religion, gender, national origin, age, familial status, or disability;

8. To refuse to consider as a valid source of income any public assistance, alimony, or child support, awarded by a court, when that source can be verified as to its amount, length of time received, regularity, or receipt because of race, color, religion, gender, national origin, age, familial status, or disability;

9. To discriminate against a person in the terms, conditions, or privileges relating to the obtaining or use of financial assistance for the acquisition, construction, rehabilitation, repair, or maintenance of any housing because of race, color, religion, gender, national origin, age, familial status, or disability;

10. To discharge, demote, or discriminate in matters of compensation or working conditions against any employee or agent because of the obedience of the employee or agent to the provisions of this section;

11. To solicit or attempt to solicit the listing of housing for sale or lease, by door to door solicitation, in person, or by telephone, or by distribution of circulars, if one of the purposes is to change the racial composition of the neighborhood;

12. To knowingly induce or attempt to induce another person to transfer an interest in real property, or to discourage another person from purchasing real property, by representations regarding the existing or potential proximity of real property owned, used, or occupied by persons of any particular race, color, religion, gender, national origin, age, familial status or disability, or to represent that such existing or potential proximity shall or may result in:

a. the lowering of property values,

b. a change in the racial, religious, or ethnic character of the block, neighborhood, or area in which the property is located,

c. an increase in criminal or antisocial behavior in the area, or

d. a decline in quality of the schools serving the area;

13. To refuse to rent or lease housing to a blind, deaf, or disabled person on the basis of the person's use or possession of a bona fide, properly trained guide, signal, or service dog;

14. To demand the payment of an additional nonrefundable fee or an unreasonable deposit for rent from a blind, deaf, or disabled person for such dog. Such blind, deaf, or disabled person may be liable for any damage done to the dwelling by such dog;

15. a. to discriminate in the sale or rental or otherwise make available or deny a dwelling to any buyer or renter because of a disability of:

(1) that buyer or renter,

(2) a person residing in or intending to reside in that dwelling after it is sold, rented, or made available, or

(3) any person associated with that buyer or renter, or

b. to discriminate against any person in the terms, conditions, or privileges of sale or rental of a dwelling or in the provision of services or facilities in connection with the dwelling because of a disability of:

(1) that person,

(2) a person residing in or intending to reside in that dwelling after it is so sold, rented, or made available, or

(3) any person associated with that person;

16. For purposes of disability discrimination in housing pursuant to Sections 1451 through 1453 of this title, discrimination includes:

a. a refusal to permit, at the expense of the disabled person, reasonable modifications of existing premises occupied or to be occupied by the person if the modifications may be necessary to afford the person full enjoyment of the premises, provided that such person also provides a surety bond guaranteeing restoration of the premises to their prior condition, if necessary to make the premises suitable for nondisabled tenants,

b. a refusal to make reasonable accommodations in rules, policies, practices, or services, when the accommodations may be necessary to afford the person equal opportunity to use and enjoy a dwelling, or

c. in connection with the design and construction of covered multifamily dwellings for first occupancy thirty (30) months after the date of enactment of the federal Fair Housing Amendments Act of 1988 (Public Law 100-430), a failure to design and construct those dwellings in a manner that:

(1) the public use and common use portions of the dwellings are readily accessible to and usable by disabled persons,

(2) all the doors designed to allow passage into and within all premises within the dwellings are sufficiently wide to allow passage by disabled persons in wheelchairs, and

(3) all premises within the dwellings contain the following features of adaptive design:

(a) an accessible route into and through the dwelling,

(b) light switches, electrical outlets, thermostats, and other environmental controls in accessible locations,

(c) reinforcements in bathroom walls to allow later installation of grab bars, and

(d) usable kitchen and bathrooms so that an individual in a wheelchair can maneuver about the space,

(4) compliance with the appropriate requirements of the American National Standard for buildings and facilities providing accessibility and usability for physically disabled people, commonly cited as "ANSI A 117.1", suffices to satisfy the requirements of division (3) of this subparagraph,

(5) as used in this subsection, the term "covered multifamily dwellings" means:

(a) buildings consisting of four or more units if the buildings have one or more elevators, and

(b) ground floor units in other buildings consisting of four or more units,

(6) nothing in this subsection requires that a dwelling be made available to an individual whose tenancy would constitute a direct threat to the health or safety of other individuals or whose tenancy would result in substantial physical damage to the property of others; or

17. a. A person whose business includes engaging in residential real estate related transactions may not discriminate against a person in making a real estate related transaction available or in the terms or conditions of a real estate related transaction because of race, color, religion, gender, disability, familial status, national origin or age.

b. In this section, "residential real estate related transaction" means:

(1) making or purchasing loans or providing other financial assistance:

(a) to purchase, construct, improve, repair, or maintain a dwelling, or

(b) to secure residential real estate, or

(2) selling, brokering, or appraising residential real property.

B. This section does not prohibit discrimination against a person because the person has been convicted under federal law or the law of any state of the illegal manufacture or distribution of a controlled substance.

C. No other categories or classes of persons are protected pursuant to Sections 1451 through 1453 of this title. The Attorney General's Office of Civil Rights Enforcement shall have no authority or jurisdiction to act on complaints based on any kind of discrimination other than those kinds of discrimination prohibited pursuant to Section 1101 et seq. of this title or any other specifically authorized by law.

§25-1453. Exemptions

A. Nothing provided for in Sections 1451 through 1453 of this title shall:

Oklahoma Fair Housing Law

1. Prohibit a religious organization, association, or society, or any nonprofit institution or organization operated, supervised, or controlled by or in conjunction with a religious organization, association, or society, from limiting the sale, rental, or occupancy of housing which it owns or operates for other than a commercial purpose to persons of the same religion, or from giving preferences to such persons, unless membership in such religion is restricted on account of race, color, or national origin. Nor shall anything in Sections 1451, 1452, 1453, 1501 and 1505.1 of this title apply to a private membership club which is a bona fide club and which is exempt from taxation pursuant to Section 501(c) of the Internal Revenue Code of 1954;

2. Prohibit a religious organization, association, or society, or a nonprofit institution or organization operated, supervised, or controlled by or in conjunction with a religious organization, association, or society, from:

a. limiting the sale, rental, or occupancy of dwellings that it owns or operates for other than a commercial purpose to persons of the same religion, or

b. giving preference to persons of the same religion, unless membership in the religion is restricted because of race, color, or national origin; or

3. Prohibit a private club not open to the public that, as an incident to its primary purpose, provides lodging that it owns or operates for other than a commercial purpose from limiting the rental or occupancy of that lodging to its members or from giving preference to its members.

B. Nothing provided for in Sections 1451 through 1453 of this title relating to familial status applies to housing for older persons. As used in this section, "housing for older persons" means housing:

1. That the Attorney General's Office of Civil Rights Enforcement determines is specifically designed and operated to assist elderly persons pursuant to a federal or state program;

2. Intended for, and solely occupied by, persons sixty-two (62) years of age or older; or

3. Intended and operated for occupancy by at least one person fifty-five (55) years of age or older per unit as determined by rules of the Attorney General's Office of Civil Rights Enforcement.

C. 1. Subject to division (2) of subparagraph a of this paragraph, Sections 1451 through 1453 of this title do not apply to:

a. the sale or rental of a single-family house sold or rented by an owner if:

(1) the owner does not:

(a) own more than three single-family houses at any one time, or

(b) own any interest in, or is there owned or reserved on his or her behalf, pursuant to any express or voluntary agreement, title to or any right to any part of the proceeds from the sale or rental of more than three single-family houses at any one time, and

(2) the house was sold or rented without:

(a) the use of the sales or rental facilities or services of a real estate broker, agent, or salesman licensed pursuant to the Oklahoma Real Estate License Code, or of an employee or agent of a licensed broker, agent, or salesman, or the facilities or services of the owner of a dwelling designed or intended for occupancy by five or more families, or

(b) the publication, posting, or mailing of a notice, statement, or advertisement prohibited by Section 1452 of this title, or

b. the sale or rental of rooms or units in a dwelling containing living quarters occupied or intended to be occupied by no more than four families living independently of each other, if the owner maintains and occupies one of the living quarters as the owner's residence.

2. The exemption in subparagraph a of paragraph 1 of this subsection applies to only one sale or rental in a twenty-four-month period, if the owner was not the most recent resident of the house at the time of the sale or rental.

D. Nothing provided for in Sections 1451 through 1453 of this title shall prohibit a person engaged in the business of furnishing appraisals of real property from taking into consideration factors other than race, color, age, religion, gender, disability, familial status, or national origin.

E. Nothing provided for in Sections 1451 through 1453 of this title shall affect a reasonable local or state restriction on the maximum number of occupants permitted to occupy a dwelling or restriction relating to health or safety standards.

F. Nothing provided for in Sections 1451 through 1453 of this title shall prevent or restrict the sale, lease, rental, transfer, or development of housing designed or intended for the use of the disabled.

G. Nothing provided for in Sections 1451 through 1453 of this title shall affect a requirement of nondiscrimination in any other state or federal law.

H. Nothing provided for in Sections 1451 through 1453 of this title shall prohibit the transfer of property by will, intestate succession, or by gift.

Oklahoma Fair Housing Law

Article 5. Attorney General's Office of Civil Rights Enforcement; Judicial Review

§25-1501. Attorney General's Office of Civil Rights Enforcement – Powers

A. Within the limitations provided by law, the Attorney General's Office of Civil Rights Enforcement has the following additional powers:

1. To promote the creation of local commissions on human rights, and to contract with individuals and state, local and other agencies, both public and private, including agencies of the federal government and of other states;

2. To accept public grants or private gifts, bequests, or other payments;

3. To receive, investigate, seek to conciliate, hold hearings on, and pass upon complaints alleging violations of Section 1101 et seq. of this title;

4. To furnish technical assistance requested by persons subject to this act to further compliance with Section 1101 et seq. of this title or an order issued thereunder;

5. To make provisions for technical and clerical assistance to an advisory committee or committees appointed in accordance with paragraph (b) of Section 953 of Title 74 of the Oklahoma Statutes;

6. To require answers to interrogatories, under the procedures established by Section 3233 of Title 12 of the Oklahoma Statutes, compel the attendance of witnesses, examine witnesses under oath or affirmation, and require the production of documents in connection with complaints filed under Section 1101 et seq. of this title, said powers to be exercised only in relation to areas directly and materially related to the complaint;

7. To hear, and issue orders on, complaints involving state government agencies and departments on the same basis as complaints involving private employers; and

8. To provide technical assistance and public information to assist in preventing and eliminating discriminatory housing practices; and

9. To promulgate rules as necessary to implement the provisions of Section 1101 et seq. of this title.

B. The Attorney General shall:

1. At least annually, publish a written report recommending legislative or other action to carry out the purposes of Section 1101 et seq. of this title as it relates to housing discrimination;

2. Make studies relating to the nature and extent of discriminatory housing practices in this state; and

3. Cooperate with and, as appropriate, may provide technical and other assistance to federal, state, local, and other public or private entities that are formulating or operating programs to prevent or eliminate discriminatory housing practices.

§25-1502. Proceedings After Complaint

A. A person claiming to be aggrieved by a discriminatory practice, his or her attorney, or a nonprofit organization chartered for the purpose of combatting discrimination may file with the Attorney General's Office of Civil Rights Enforcement a written sworn complaint stating that a discriminatory practice has been committed, and setting forth the facts upon which the complaint is based, and setting forth facts sufficient to enable the Attorney General to identify the person charged, hereinafter called the respondent. The Attorney General shall promptly furnish the respondent with a copy of the complaint and shall promptly investigate the allegations of discriminatory practice set forth in the complaint. The complaint must be filed within one hundred eighty (180) days after the alleged discriminatory practice occurs.

B. If within sixty (60) days after the complaint is filed it is determined by the Attorney General that there is no reasonable cause to believe that the respondent has engaged in a discriminatory practice, the Attorney General shall issue an order dismissing the complaint and shall furnish a copy of the order to the complainant, the respondent and such other public officers and persons as the Attorney General deems proper.

C. The complainant, within thirty (30) days after receiving a copy of an order dismissing the complaint, may file with the Attorney General an application for reconsideration of the order. Upon such application, the Attorney General shall make a new determination whether there is a reasonable cause to believe that the respondent has engaged in a discriminatory practice. If it is determined within thirty (30) days after the application is filed that there is no reasonable cause to believe that the respondent has engaged in a discriminatory practice, the Attorney General shall issue an order dismissing the complaint and furnish a copy of the order to the complainant, the respondent and such other public officers as the Attorney General deems proper.

D. This section does not apply to persons claiming to be aggrieved by a discriminatory housing practice to the extent that it is inconsistent with specific provisions of Section 1101 et seq. of this title relating to a discriminatory housing complaint.

§25-1502.1. Temporary Injunctive Relief and Restraining Order

If, at any time after the receipt of a verified charge, the Attorney General has reason to believe that a respondent has engaged in any unlawful discriminatory practice, the Attorney General may file a petition in the district court in a county in which the subject of the complaint occurs, or in a county in which a respondent resides or transacts business, seeking appropriate temporary injunctive relief against the respondent pending final determination of proceedings pursuant to Section 1101 et seq. of this title. The court shall have power to grant injunctive relief or a restraining order as it deems just and proper, but no relief or order shall be granted except by consent of the respondent or after hearing upon notice to the respondent and a finding by the court that there is reasonable cause to believe that the respondent has engaged in a discriminatory practice. Except as modified by this section, the Oklahoma rules of civil procedure shall apply to an application, and the district court shall have authority to grant or deny the relief sought on conditions as it deems just and equitable. This section is subject to the provisions of Section 1502.7 of this title.

§25-1502.2. Investigation of Alleged Discriminatory Housing Practices - Form of Complaint – Procedure

A. The Attorney General shall investigate alleged discriminatory housing practices.
B. A complaint must be:
1. In writing;
2. Under oath; and
3. In the form prescribed by the Attorney General.
C. An aggrieved person may, not later than one (1) year after an alleged discriminatory housing practice has occurred or terminated, whichever is later, file a complaint with the Attorney General alleging the discriminatory housing practice.
D. Not later than one (1) year after an alleged discriminatory housing practice has occurred or terminated, whichever is later, the Attorney General may file his or her own complaint.
E. A complaint may be amended at any time.
F. On the filing of a complaint the Attorney General shall:
1. Give the aggrieved person notice that the complaint has been received;
2. Advise the aggrieved person of the time limits and choice of forums pursuant to Section 1101 et seq. of this title; and
3. Not later than the 20th day after the filing of the complaint or the identification of an additional respondent pursuant to Section 1502.5 of this title, serve on each respondent:
a. a notice identifying the alleged discriminatory housing practice and advising the respondent of the procedural rights and obligations of a respondent pursuant to Section 1101 et seq. of this title, and
b. a copy of the original complaint.

§25-1502.3. Answer to the Complaint

A. Not later than the 10th day after receipt of the notice and copy pursuant to paragraph 3 of subsection F of Section 1502.2 of this title, a respondent may file an answer to the complaint.
B. An answer must be:
1. In writing;
2. Under oath; and
3. In the form prescribed by the Attorney General.
C. An answer may be amended at any time.
D. An answer does not inhibit the investigation of a complaint.

§25-1502.4. Complaint Referral From Federal Government and Investigation

If the federal government has referred a complaint to the Attorney General or has deferred jurisdiction over the subject matter of the complaint to the Attorney General, the Attorney General shall promptly investigate the allegations set forth in the complaint.

§25-1502.5. Joinder

A. The Commission may join a person not named in the complaint as an additional or substitute respondent if in the course of the investigation the Commission determines that the person should be accused of a discriminatory housing practice.
B. In addition to the information required in the notice pursuant to paragraph 3 of subsection F of Section 8 of this act, the Commission shall include in a notice to a respondent joined pursuant to this section an explanation of the basis for the determination that the person is properly joined as a respondent.

§25-1502.6. Complaint Conciliation

A. The Attorney General may, during the period beginning with the filing of a complaint and ending with the filing of a charge or a dismissal by the Attorney General's Office of Civil Rights Enforcement, to the extent feasible, engage in conciliation with respect to the complaint.
B. A conciliation agreement is an agreement between a respondent and the complainant and is subject to the Attorney General's approval.
C. A conciliation agreement may provide for binding arbitration or other method of dispute resolution. Dispute resolution that results from a conciliation agreement may authorize appropriate relief, including monetary relief.
D. A conciliation agreement shall be made public unless the complainant and respondent agree otherwise, and the Attorney General determines that disclosure is not necessary to further the purpose of Section 1101 et seq. of this title.
E. Nothing said or done in the course of conciliation may be made public or used as evidence in a subsequent proceeding pursuant to Section 1101 et seq. of this title without the written consent of the persons concerned.
F. After completion of any investigation conducted by the Attorney General, the Attorney General shall make available to the aggrieved person and the respondent, at any time, information derived from the investigation and the final investigation report relating to that investigation.

§25-1502.7. Civil Action for Appropriate Temporary or Preliminary Relief

A. If the Attorney General concludes at any time following the filing of a discriminatory housing complaint that prompt judicial action is necessary to carry out the purposes of Section 1101 et seq. of this title, the Attorney General may commence a civil action for appropriate temporary or preliminary relief pending final disposition of the complaint.
B. A temporary restraining order or other order granting preliminary or temporary relief on a discriminatory housing complaint filed under this section is governed by the provisions of Section 1502.1 of this title and the applicable Oklahoma rules of civil procedure.

§25-1502.15. Civil Action By Attorney General on Behalf of the Aggrieved Person

A. The Attorney General may file a civil action on behalf of the aggrieved person in a district court seeking relief pursuant to this section.
B. Venue for an action pursuant to this section is in the county in which the alleged discriminatory housing practice occurred, or in a county where the respondent resides or transacts business.
C. An aggrieved person may intervene in the action.
D. If the court finds that a discriminatory housing practice has occurred or is about to occur, the court may grant as relief any relief that a court may grant in a civil action pursuant to Section 1506.3 of this title.
E. If monetary relief is sought for the benefit of an aggrieved person who does not intervene in the civil action, the court may not award the monetary relief if that aggrieved person has not complied with discovery orders entered by the court.

Oklahoma Fair Housing Law

§25-1505.1. Certification of Attorney General's Determination of Housing Discrimination

If the Attorney General upon final determination finds that an act of housing discrimination pursuant to Section 1452 of this title has been committed by a person holding a real estate license pursuant to state law, the Attorney General will certify such determination to the licensing agency. Unless such determination of discriminatory practice is reversed in the course of judicial review, a final determination is binding on the licensing agency. Such agency shall take appropriate administrative action, including suspension or revocation of the license of the respondent.

§25-1506.1. Civil Action

A. An aggrieved person may file a civil action in district court not later than the second year after the occurrence of the termination of an alleged discriminatory housing practice, or the breach of a conciliation agreement entered into pursuant to Section 1101 et seq. of this title, whichever occurs last, to obtain appropriate relief with respect to the discriminatory housing practice or breach.
B. The two-year period does not include any time during which an administrative hearing pursuant to Section 1101 et seq. of this title is pending with respect to a complaint or charge pursuant to Section 1101 et seq. of this title based on the discriminatory housing practice. This subsection does not apply to actions arising from a breach of a conciliation agreement.
C. An aggrieved person may file an action pursuant to this section whether or not a complaint has been filed pursuant to Section 1502.2 of this title and without regard to the status of any complaint filed pursuant to this section.
D. If the Attorney General has obtained a conciliation agreement with the consent of an aggrieved person, the aggrieved person may not file an action pursuant to this section with respect to the alleged discriminatory housing practice that forms the basis for the complaint except to enforce the terms of the agreement.
E. An aggrieved person may not file an action pursuant to this section with respect to an alleged discriminatory housing practice that forms the basis of a charge issued by the Attorney General if the Attorney General has begun a hearing on the record pursuant to Section 1101 et seq. of this title with respect to the charge.

§25-1506.2. Court May Appoint An Attorney

On application by a person alleging a discriminatory housing practice or by a person against whom such a practice is alleged, the court may appoint an attorney for the person.

§25-1506.3. Remedies Available to the Court

In an action pursuant to Section 1101 et seq. of this title, if the court finds that a discriminatory housing practice has occurred or is about to occur, the court may award to the plaintiff:
1. Actual and punitive damages;
2. Reasonable attorney fees;
3. Court costs; and
4. Subject to Section 1506.4 of this title, any permanent or temporary injunction, temporary restraining order, or other order, including an order enjoining the defendant from engaging in the practice or ordering appropriate affirmative action.

§25-1506.4. Effect of Relief

Relief granted pursuant to Section 1506.3 of this title does not affect a contract, sale, encumbrance, or lease that:
1. Was consummated before the granting of the relief; and
2. Involved a bona fide purchaser, encumbrancer, or tenant who did not have actual notice of the filing of a complaint pursuant to Section 1101 et seq. of this title or a civil action pursuant to this section.

§25-1506.6. Civil Action for Appropriate Relief – Intervention

A. On request of the Commission, the Attorney General may file a civil action in district court for appropriate relief if the Commission has reasonable cause to believe that:
1. a person is engaged in pattern or practice of resistance to the full enjoyment of any right granted by this act; or

2. a person has been denied any right granted by this act and that denial raises an issue of general public importance.

B. In an action pursuant to this section the court may:

1. award preventive relief, including a permanent or temporary injunctive, restraining order, or other order against the person responsible for a violation of this act as necessary to assure the full enjoyment of the rights granted by this act;

2. award other appropriate relief, including monetary damages, reasonable attorneys fees, and court costs; and

3. to vindicate the public interest, assess a civil penalty against the respondent in an amount that does not exceed:

a. Fifty Thousand Dollars ($50,000.00), for a first violation, and

b. One Hundred Thousand Dollars ($100,000.00), for a second or subsequent violation.

C. A person may intervene in an action pursuant to this section if the person is:

1. an aggrieved person to the discriminatory housing practice; or

2. a party to a conciliation agreement concerning the discriminatory housing practice.

§25-1506.7. Subpoena

The Attorney General may issue subpoenas pursuant to Section 1101 et seq. of this title and may enforce the subpoena in appropriate proceedings in district court.

§25-1506.8. Reasonable Attorney Fees

A court in a civil action brought pursuant to Section 1101 ct seq. of this title may award reasonable attorney fees to the prevailing party and assess court costs against the nonprevailing party.

§25-1506.9. Misdemeanor Violation

A. A person commits an offense if the person, whether or not acting under color of law, by force or threat of force, intentionally intimidates or interferes with a person:

1. Because of the person's race, color, religion, gender, disability, familial status, or national origin and because the person is or has been selling, purchasing, renting, financing, occupying, contracting, or negotiating for the sale, purchase, rental, financing, or occupation of any dwelling, or applying for or participating in a service, organization, or facility relating to the business of selling or renting dwellings; or

2. Because the person is or has been, or has attempted to intimidate the person from:

a. participating, without discrimination because of race, color, religion, gender, disability, familial status, or national origin, in an activity, service, organization, or facility described in paragraph 1 of this subsection,

b. affording another person opportunity or protection to so participate, or

c. lawfully aiding or encouraging other persons to participate, without discrimination because of race, color, religion, gender, disability, familial status, or national origin, in an activity, service, organization, or facility described in paragraph 1 of this subsection.

B. An offense pursuant to this section is a misdemeanor.

§25-1507. Inspection - Records

A. In connection with an investigation of a complaint filed under Section 1101 et seq. of this title, the Attorney General shall have access at any reasonable time to premises, records and documents relevant to the complaint and the right to examine, photograph and copy evidence, in accordance with the Oklahoma Administrative Procedures Act.

B. So as to avoid undue burden on persons subject to the act, records and reports required by the Attorney General under this section shall conform as near as may be to similar records and reports required by federal law.

C. It is unlawful for an officer or employee of the Attorney General to make public with respect to a particular person without his consent information obtained by the Attorney General pursuant to his or her authority under this section.

§25-1508. Subpoenas – Witnesses

A. Subpoenas shall issue in proceedings under Section 1101 et seq. of this title as provided in the Oklahoma Administrative Procedures Act. A subpoena so issued shall show on its face the name and address of the party at whose request the subpoena was issued. On petition of the individual to whom the subpoena is directed and notice to the requesting party, the Attorney General may vacate or modify the subpoena.

B. Witnesses whose depositions are taken or who are summoned before the Attorney General or employees of the Attorney General's office shall be entitled to the same witness and mileage fees as are paid to witnesses in the courts of the state.

Made in the USA
Columbia, SC
14 February 2019